橘　由加 監修・編著
Linc Educational Resources, Inc 編

オンライン英語学習用テキスト

# lincEnglish
# Gold I

大学教育出版

# はじめに

　本書は Linc Educational Resources, Inc. が開発した、総合的英語力を伸ばすオンライン学習システム Linc English の GoldⅠ（レベル表参照）のコンテンツをテキスト用に編集したものです。Linc English はリスニング、リーディング、文法・語彙、ライティングの総合的英語能力をのばすためのオンライン英語学習教材です。また、英検および TOEFL、TOEIC、センター試験のスコア・アップのために、聴解、読解、文法・語彙、筆記の能力養成教材としても有効です。この総合英語カリキュラムで学習することにより、ハイレベルな英語力の向上を狙います。留学準備、大学や大学院入学対策にもなります。カリキュラムは中1年生（英検5級程度）から上級までのレベルで構成されており、多量のコンテンツを学習することにより、総合的な英語力を身につけることを目標としています。

　日本人の英語学習者に不足しているのは、①英語を聞き続ける「持久力」、②英語で即反応できる「瞬発力」の2つの力です。また学習量、学習時間が不足しているため、読解力、聴解力の弱さが目立ちます。学校の現場では、①教科書だけで徹底的に鍛えることが難しい、②多量の宿題を出しても、採点する時間がない、③授業以外で十分な時間をとることが難しい、などが現状ではないでしょうか。このような問題を解決するためには、授業＋セルフスタディーの学習リズムを作る必要があります。そこで開発されたのが Linc English です。本書 GoldⅠ は、TOEIC：450〜600、TOEFL（PBT）：460〜500、（CBT）：140〜173、英検2級レベルの学習者を対象としています。

　Linc English のコンセプトデザインは、①カリキュラム・ティーム、②システム、③コンテンツの3つから成り立っています。学習するコンテンツはすべて、現役のアメリカ人コラムニストや ESL の専門家が日本人のために作成した完全オリジナルです。音声は、リスニング問題はもちろん、リーディング問題にも収録されています。インターネットを活用するので、学校でも家でも学習することができ、学習者は都合に合わせて演習に取り組むことができます。採点は自動的に行われるので、教師の採点作業が一切不要になります。学習時間、到達度、評価などをパソコンで把握できます（自動採点システム、学習管理機能システム搭載）。膨大なコンテンツ量で、年間24レッスンをカリキュラムとした場合、演習時間をテキストに書き出すと A4 判にしておよそ 2,500 ページにもなりますが、コンテンツの量や難易度を調整し、アップデートをしていくことができます。

　Linc English オンライン・カリキュラムはトータルで216レッスン、28,000以上の演習問題、A4判で18,000ページにもおよぶ莫大なコンテンツ量です。レベルは Pre Bronze（Ⅰ, Ⅱ）、Bronze（Ⅰ, Ⅱ, Ⅲ）、Silver（Ⅰ, Ⅱ, Ⅲ）Gold（Ⅰ, Ⅱ, Ⅲ）、Platinum A（Ⅰ, Ⅱ, Ⅲ）、Platinum B（Ⅰ, Ⅱ, Ⅲ）から構成されています。Linc English は個人別・能力別に学習者のレベルに合わせ、自分のペースで学習を進めることができます。リスニング、リーディング教材のトピックはショート・ストーリー、エッセイ、文芸、芸術、歴史、異文化、政治・経済、世界情勢、ニュース、情報、環境、スポーツ、哲学、論説文など多岐にわたっています。教材はやさしい段階から少しず

つ高度な内容へと17レベル構成になっています。

　自分のペースで何回でも演習できるので、確実に英語力をのばしたい学習者にとっては、絶対必須のカリキュラムです。またオンライン上で学習管理が容易にできるので、英語力がどのように上達しているか把握できます。英語力をつけるには毎日数時間の集中学習が必要です。語学学習は演習量がものをいいます。興味深いコンテンツで膨大な演習問題をこなしていく、そんな学習法が英語教育では必要ではないでしょうか。

　学校の先生方にはLinc Englishを是非CALL授業でお使いになることをお勧めします。英語のカリキュラムの一環として授業と連動させながら、補足教材としてLinc Englishで指導することもできるでしょう。コンテンツを本書のようにテキスト化した理由は、教師・学習者がコンピュータルーム以外でも、一般の英語の授業で使えるようにするためです。また自宅にインターネット環境のパソコンがない場合は、学校でパソコンで演習し、自宅ではテキストで学習できます。授業でLinc Englishをお使いになる場合の授業プラン、指導案も「本書の構成と活用法」で簡単に説明いたしますので、参考にしていただければ幸いです。CALL授業のカリキュラムに何かのプログラムをすでに導入されている場合は、学習者個人の自主学習教材として利用していただくこともできます。アメリカの大学留学のためのTOEFL対策、就職準備や英語力向上のため、TOEICのスコアを上げたい学習者にとって、Linc Englishは最適なオンライン学習教材です。

　最後になりますが、問題作成に協力していただいたLinc Englishカリキュラム・ティームの皆様に感謝の意を表したいと思います。なお、本書の製作にあたっては、大学教育出版代表の佐藤守氏、および三好弘明氏から多大な協力を頂きました。末筆になりましたが、この場を借りて改めてお礼を申し上げます。

2008年9月3日

監修者・編著者　橘　由加

# 本書の構成と効果的な活用法

　本書は12レッスンからなり、各レッスンは7種のプラクティス演習で構成されています。これを（Part）とよびます。本書は、Linc Englishのデジタルコンテンツの演習問題と解説をテキスト用に編集してまとめたものです。学習者の自宅学習のテキストとして、また学校の授業でも使えるように配慮しています。以下にカリキュラム概要、オンライン教材と本書を併用した授業プラン（指導案）を説明します。

## Linc Englishカリキュラムの概要

* 学生、高校生、大学生、社会人を対象とした総合英語学習カリキュラムです。
* 英語の4技能（リスニング、リーディング、ライティング、スピーキング）の発達を目指します。
* 英検、TOEIC、TOEFLの対策や受験英語、ビジネス英語、英語教員養成英語など、さまざまな用途別のオンライン英語学習とも連結しています。
* レベルは全部で6レベル。やさしい内容から少しずつ高度な内容へと17セクションの構成になっており、個人別・能力別に学習者のレベルに合わせ、自分のペースで学習することができます。
* リスニングやリーディング教材のトピックは、エッセイ、芸術、文芸、政治・経済、世界情勢など多岐にわたっています。
* 授業プランや指導用のマニュアルも用意しており、通常の対面型授業を補完する学習システムとして利用できます。またレベルごとのテキストブックも揃えており、他のオンライン学習システムと大きく異なるところです。

## 教材のレベルと学習対象者

　Linc Englishは、Pre Bronze（Ⅰ, Ⅱ）、Bronze（Ⅰ, Ⅱ, Ⅲ）、Silver（Ⅰ, Ⅱ, Ⅲ）、Gold（Ⅰ, Ⅱ, Ⅲ）、Platinum A（Ⅰ, Ⅱ, Ⅲ）、Platinum B（Ⅰ, Ⅱ, Ⅲ）、の全部で6レベルから構成され、17セクションに分かれています。中学1年生から英語教育者・上級レベルの社会人まで、豊富なラインアップとなっています。中学生の場合は1年間の授業で18レッスン、高校生から大学生の場合は1年間で24レッスンで終了できるような指導をお勧めします。

| 17 Levels & Standards | Grade | Score |
| --- | --- | --- |
| Pre Bronze Ⅰ, Ⅱ | 中学生（初級・低） | TOEIC: 50～150（TOEICブリッジ: 20～180）／TOEFL: PBT 300～350　CBT 20～63／英検: 5級・4級 |
| Bronze Ⅰ, Ⅱ, Ⅲ | 中学3年生・高校生（初級・高） | TOEIC: 200～300／TOEFL: PBT 350～400　CBT 63～97／英検: 3級・準2級 |
| Silver Ⅰ, Ⅱ, Ⅲ | 高校3年生・大学生（中級・低） | TOEIC: 300～450／TOEFL: PBT 400～460　CBT 97～140／英検: 準2級・2級 |
| Gold Ⅰ, Ⅱ, Ⅲ | 大学生（中級・高） | TOEIC: 450～600／TOEFL: PBT 460～500　CBT 140～173／英検: 2級・準1級 |
| Platinum A Ⅰ, Ⅱ, Ⅲ | 大学生・一般・ビジネスマン（上級） | TOEIC: 600～800／TOEFL: PBT 500～570　CBT 173～230／英検: 準1級 |
| Platinum B Ⅰ, Ⅱ, Ⅲ | 大学生・英語教育者（上級） | TOEIC: 800～990／TOEFL: PBT 570～677　CBT 173～300／英検: 1級 |

* レベルと対象学習者はあくまでも目安です。学習者の能力や必要に応じて、レベルを選べます。
* 児童、小学生、児童英語教育関係者対象のLinc Kids Englishもございます。

## Linc Englishオンライン・カリキュラム（レッスンの構造）

| 種別 | 内容 | 問題数 |
|---|---|---|
| リスニング | 写真描写問題 | 25 問 |
| | 質疑応答問題 | 30 問 |
| | 会話問題 | 30 問 |
| | 説明文問題 | 10 問 |
| リーディング | 段落速読問題 | 12 問 |
| | 読解問題 | 4 問 |
| | 文脈問題 | 3 問 |
| グラマー＆ボキャブラリー | 空所補充問題 | 40 問 |
| | 誤文訂正問題 | 25 問 |
| レッスン合計 | | 179 問 |

※Bronze～Goldの例

## Linc Englishテキスト構成

- Part I　Image Listening／写真描写問題
- Part II　Question and Response／質疑応答問題
- Part III　Short Conversation／会話問題
- Part IV　Short Talks／説明文問題
- Part V　Reading／読解問題
- Part VI　Error Recognition／空所補充問題
- Part VII　Incomplete Sentence／文法・語彙問題

＊　テキストには、リーディング・セクションの段落速読問題と文脈問題は掲載していません。
＊　問題も抜粋して、順序を変えています。

## オンラインでの演習所要時間の目安

　各レベルの演習所要時間はあくまで目安です。セルフ・スタディーでは、1レッスンを1週間かけて終了するつもりで、何回も演習を繰り返してください。毎日最低でも1時間以上の学習を目標にすると、英語力がついてきます。先生方には学校でLinc Englishを導入して授業で利用する場合、各レッスンを2週間かけて終了することをお勧めします。またテキストを使って自宅学習、筆記の宿題も出すことができます。授業用に20分ほどのクイズも用意していますので、最初の1週目の授業でレッスンのポイントや演習のコツを学ばせ、2週目の授業でクイズをし、答え合わせや解説を行うなど、いろいろと工夫のある授業が考えられます。

　＊以下に記す授業の進め方、授業モデルを参照

### （1）中学生対象：プリ・ブロンズのオンライン演習とテキスト構成

　プリ・ブロンズは、各レッスン6種のプラクティス（演習）から構成されており、テキストではプラクティスを6種（part）としています。テキストはオンライン演習と同じ内容ですが、教材の一部の演習問題と解説を編集してテキスト用にまとめています。

●リスニング・セクション：4種のプラクティス（テキストではPart）
　1．写真描写問題　　15問　（時間約8分）
　2．質疑応答問題　　20問　（10分）

3．会話問題　　　　　15問　（8分）
　　4．説明文問題　　　　10問　（12分）
●リーディングセクション：1種のプラクティス
　　5．読解問題　　　　　4～5段落　5問　（時間約10分）
●文法・語彙セクション：1種のプラクティス
　　6．空所補充問題　　　25問　（時間15分）

*各レッスンを約60分で終了させることを目標とする

（2）　**高校・大学生対象：ブロンズ～ゴールドのオンライン演習とテキスト構成**
　　ブロンズ～ゴールドは、各レッスン9種のプラクティス（演習）から構成されていますが、テキストではプラクティスを7種（Part）としています。テキストはオンライン演習と同じ内容ですが、教材の一部の演習問題と解説を編集してテキスト用にまとめています。
●**リスニングセクション：4種のプラクティス（テキストではPart）**
　　1．描写問題　　　　　25問　（時間約12分）
　　2．質疑応答問題　　　30問　（時間約12分）
　　3．会話問題　　　　　30問　（時間約12分）
　　4．説明文問題　　　　10問　（時間約12分）
●**リーディングセクション：　3種のプラクティスであるが段落問題と読解問題の本文は同じ内容**
　　5．段落速読問題（時間制限有り）　　4段落　12問　（時間約7分）　テキストには載せていない
　　6．読解問題　　　　　4段落　　　　4問　（時間約10分）
　　7．文脈問題　　　　　2～3段落　　3問　（時間約6分）　テキストには載せていない
●**文法・語彙セクション：2種のプラクティス**
　　1．空所補充問題　　　40問　（時間約20分）
　　2．誤文訂正問題　　　25問　（時間約12分）

*各レッスンを約100分で終了させることを目標とする

（3）　**大学生・社会人対象：プラティナのオンライン演習教材とテキスト構成**
　　プラティナは、各レッスン6種のプラクティス（演習）から構成されていますが、テキストではプラクティスを5種（Part）としています。テキストはオンライン演習と同じ内容ですが、教材の一部の演習問題と解説を編集してテキスト用にまとめています。
●**リスニンググセクション：1種のプラクティス（テキストではPart）**
　　1．説明文問題　　　　10問　（時間約12～15分）
●**リーディングセクション：3種のプラクティス**
　　2．段落速読問題　　（時間制限有り）　4段落　12問　（時間約　7分）　テキストには載せていない
　　3．読解問題　　　　　4段落　　　　4問　（時間約15分）
　　4．文脈問題　　　　　2～3段落　　3問　（時間約7分）　テキストには載せていない
●**文法・語彙セクション：2種のプラクティス**
　　5．空所補充問題題　20問　（10分）
　　6．誤文訂正問題　　12問　（8分）

*各レッスンを約60分で終了させることを目標とする

## 本書（Gold I）を併用したLinc English授業モデル＜大学生レベル＞

英語の授業を円滑に進めるためには、最低限度の英語運用能力、「読む、書く、聞く、話す」という4技能と「文法、発音、語彙」の3領域の充実が求められますが、特に文法、語彙という形式操作能力とリーディング、リスニングという受容能力（インプット）の訓練が強く求められます。よく「会話力」の向上を求める声が高まっていますが、リスニングと文法・語彙を確実にすることで、初めてコミュニケーション能力が育成されます。このようなことから、学習者個人の能力に合わせた最適な環境、いわゆる自主学習を通して基礎力の補強を支援するCALL教育が必要となります。CALLは、本来個別学習を特色としますが、教室内外で学習者が自分のペースで学習を進めていくことが可能です。

### （1）授業環境
① 授業時には、教員が指導にあたりますが、コンピュータの技術的サポートは学内の技術員が担当するものとする。
② CALL設定されているコンピュータの操作は、学生証によってログオンするか、各自に与えられたパスワードの入力によるか、いずれかの手続きでログオンすれば、教材を直ちにサーバーから取り込むことができる。
③ 授業形態は1コマ90分とし、決められたシラバスに準じて学習を進められるが、進度は各自のペースで自由に学習する。また課題学習が毎回出される。
④ CALL教室の空き時間には、学習者が空き時間を利用して自主的に補習することができる態勢を整える。

### （2）授業の進め方
① シラバスで学習教材の順序を周知させた上で、自由に学習を進めさせます。学習者側の責任で学習を進めていくため、習熟度により自由に学習を展開させることが可能で、学習者に満足感を与えることができます。
② 毎時間、シラバス通りに学習すべきレッスンを指定します。授業時間内にレッスンを終了できないとき、あるいは授業を欠席したときなどは、次週の授業時間までにレッスンを各自終了させておくことを義務づけます。シラバス通りに学習を進めていくため、学習者が同じ範囲を学習しますが、進度の速い人でもレッスンごとに十分な質問問題が用意されているため、時間を無駄にすることはありません。詳しくは、Linc Englishのカリキュラムの概要に教材内容、レッスン構成、問題数と流れの説明があるので参照してください。またLinc EnglishのＨＰにアクセスして、トライアルにログインすると体験できるので問題構成を把握できます。

### （3）授業モデル
① はじめの5分で、テキストでその日の授業でカバーする演習（テキストでは〈Part〉とよぶ）のポイントや重要な英語表現のまとめをひと通り確認する（教師による一斉指導）。
② 次の5分で、今確認した知識をLinc Englishで（1講座コンテンツ）試す。
③ 次の3分で、今の②の解答を確認。
④ 次の5分で、上の②のLinc Englishに出てきた単語や語句、または文法事項をテキストで再度確認する（教師による一斉指導）。
⑤ 次の5分で、テキストのドリル問題に取り組ませて定着させる（この⑤の間、教師は巡回個別指導を行う）。
このような23分×2サイクル（2講座）を1回の授業とします。

**（速読読解練習の例）**

　オンラインの速読問題は、10行程度の文章に3問×4段落という構造になっていますので、その全体を7分程度で読み終えるようにします（カウントダウン制御機能があります）。授業ではテキストを利用して、10行程度の文章に2問、1段落のみを2分程度で読み終えるよう速度練習させます。次の演習として、10行程の文章に1問×4段落という全体を4分程度で読み終えるようにします。このような演習を繰り返すことで速読の力がつきます。この速読演習のあとに、読解演習にはいると、効果が期待できます。

**（4）学習の評価**

　クイズやテストなどの結果の評価とともに、学習評価過程を評価することも重要です。常に学習目標や授業展開にフィードバックしていなければなりません。Linc Englishでは自己評価シートが作成できます。また学習過程の成果もファイルできます。教員もクラスごとに学習者の学習過程を把握できるし、Linc Englishの学習管理システムを利用してシラバスの情報、課題スケジュールの変更などのアナウンスメントもできるので非常に便利です。

　以上がLinc Englishのカリキュラム概要・構成と本書の効果的な活用法です。しっかりとした英語運用能力を身につけるために、Linc Englishオンライン演習と本書を併用した学習を読者の皆様に強くお勧めします。また、一読だけではなく、自分に必要なところを再度選んで何回か学習を繰り返してみてください。

---

各レッスンの Part 1 Image Listening については、下記アドレスにアクセスし、音声を聞いて問題に答えてください。
http://audio.lincenglish.com

---

オンライン英語学習用テキスト
Linc English　GOLD I

**目　次**

はじめに ……………………………………………………………………………………… i

本書の構成と効果的な使用法 ………………………………………………………………… iii

## lesson 1

| Part 1 | Image Listening／写真描写問題 …………………………………… | 1 |
| Part 2 | Question and Response／質疑応答問題 …………………………… | 2 |
| Part 3 | Short Conversation／会話問題 …………………………………… | 3 |
| Part 4 | Short Talks／説明文問題 ………………………………………… | 5 |
| Part 5 | Reading／読解演習 ………………………………………………… | 7 |
| Part 6 | Error Recognition／誤文訂正問題 ………………………………… | 10 |
| Part 7 | Incomplete Sentence／文法・語彙問題 …………………………… | 12 |

## lesson 2

| Part 1 | Image Listening／写真描写問題 …………………………………… | 13 |
| Part 2 | Question and Response／質疑応答問題 …………………………… | 14 |
| Part 3 | Short Conversation／会話問題 …………………………………… | 15 |
| Part 4 | Short Talks／説明文問題 ………………………………………… | 17 |
| Part 5 | Reading／読解演習 ………………………………………………… | 19 |
| Part 6 | Error Recognition／誤文訂正問題 ………………………………… | 22 |
| Part 7 | Incomplete Sentence／文法・語彙問題 …………………………… | 24 |

## lesson 3

| Part 1 | Image Listening／写真描写問題 …………………………………… | 25 |
| Part 2 | Question and Response／質疑応答問題 …………………………… | 26 |
| Part 3 | Short Conversation／会話問題 …………………………………… | 27 |
| Part 4 | Short Talks／説明文問題 ………………………………………… | 29 |
| Part 5 | Reading／読解演習 ………………………………………………… | 31 |
| Part 6 | Error Recognition／誤文訂正問題 ………………………………… | 33 |
| Part 7 | Incomplete Sentence／文法・語彙問題 …………………………… | 35 |

## lesson 4

| Part 1 | Image Listening／写真描写問題 …………………………………… | 36 |
| Part 2 | Question and Response／質疑応答問題 …………………………… | 37 |
| Part 3 | Short Conversation／会話問題 …………………………………… | 38 |
| Part 4 | Short Talks／説明文問題 ………………………………………… | 40 |
| Part 5 | Reading／読解演習 ………………………………………………… | 42 |
| Part 6 | Error Recognition／誤文訂正問題 ………………………………… | 44 |
| Part 7 | Incomplete Sentence／文法・語彙問題 …………………………… | 46 |

## lesson 5

| | | |
|---|---|---:|
| Part 1 | Image Listening ／写真描写問題 | *47* |
| Part 2 | Question and Response ／質疑応答問題 | *48* |
| Part 3 | Short Conversation ／会話問題 | *49* |
| Part 4 | Short Talks ／説明文問題 | *51* |
| Part 5 | Reading ／読解演習 | *53* |
| Part 6 | Error Recognition ／誤文訂正問題 | *55* |
| Part 7 | Incomplete Sentence ／文法・語彙問題 | *57* |

## lesson 6

| | | |
|---|---|---:|
| Part 1 | Image Listening ／写真描写問題 | *59* |
| Part 2 | Question and Response ／質疑応答問題 | *60* |
| Part 3 | Short Conversation ／会話問題 | *61* |
| Part 4 | Short Talks ／説明文問題 | *63* |
| Part 5 | Reading ／読解演習 | *64* |
| Part 6 | Error Recognition ／誤文訂正問題 | *67* |
| Part 7 | Incomplete Sentence ／文法・語彙問題 | *69* |

## lesson 7

| | | |
|---|---|---:|
| Part 1 | Image Listening ／写真描写問題 | *71* |
| Part 2 | Question and Response ／質疑応答問題 | *72* |
| Part 3 | Short Conversation ／会話問題 | *74* |
| Part 4 | Short Talks ／説明文問題 | *76* |
| Part 5 | Reading ／読解演習 | *78* |
| Part 6 | Error Recognition ／誤文訂正問題 | *81* |
| Part 7 | Incomplete Sentence ／文法・語彙問題 | *83* |

## lesson 8

| | | |
|---|---|---:|
| Part 1 | Image Listening ／写真描写問題 | *84* |
| Part 2 | Question and Response ／質疑応答問題 | *85* |
| Part 3 | Short Conversation ／会話問題 | *86* |
| Part 4 | Short Talks ／説明文問題 | *88* |
| Part 5 | Reading ／読解演習 | *90* |
| Part 6 | Error Recognition ／誤文訂正問題 | *92* |
| Part 7 | Incomplete Sentence ／文法・語彙問題 | *94* |

## lesson 9

- Part 1　Image Listening／写真描写問題 ･･････････････････････････････････････････ *95*
- Part 2　Question and Response／質疑応答問題 ･･･････････････････････････････ *96*
- Part 3　Short Conversation／会話問題 ･････････････････････････････････････････ *98*
- Part 4　Short Talks／説明文問題 ････････････････････････････････････････････････ *100*
- Part 5　Reading／読解演習 ･････････････････････････････････････････････････････ *102*
- Part 6　Error Recognition／誤文訂正問題 ･････････････････････････････････････ *104*
- Part 7　Incomplete Sentence／文法・語彙問題 ･･･････････････････････････････ *106*

## lesson 10

- Part 1　Image Listening／写真描写問題 ･･････････････････････････････････････････ *107*
- Part 2　Question and Response／質疑応答問題 ･･･････････････････････････････ *108*
- Part 3　Short Conversation／会話問題 ･････････････････････････････････････････ *109*
- Part 4　Short Talks／説明文問題 ････････････････････････････････････････････････ *111*
- Part 5　Reading／読解演習 ･････････････････････････････････････････････････････ *113*
- Part 6　Error Recognition／誤文訂正問題 ･････････････････････････････････････ *115*
- Part 7　Incomplete Sentence／文法・語彙問題 ･･･････････････････････････････ *117*

## lesson 11

- Part 1　Image Listening／写真描写問題 ･･････････････････････････････････････････ *119*
- Part 2　Question and Response／質疑応答問題 ･･･････････････････････････････ *120*
- Part 3　Short Conversation／会話問題 ･････････････････････････････････････････ *122*
- Part 4　Short Talks／説明文問題 ････････････････････････････････････････････････ *124*
- Part 5　Reading／読解演習 ･････････････････････････････････････････････････････ *126*
- Part 6　Error Recognition／誤文訂正問題 ･････････････････････････････････････ *128*
- Part 7　Incomplete Sentence／文法・語彙問題 ･･･････････････････････････････ *130*

## lesson 12

- Part 1　Image Listening／写真描写問題 ･･････････････････････････････････････････ *131*
- Part 2　Question and Response／質疑応答問題 ･･･････････････････････････････ *132*
- Part 3　Short Conversation／会話問題 ･････････････････････････････････････････ *134*
- Part 4　Short Talks／説明文問題 ････････････････････････････････････････････････ *136*
- Part 5　Reading／読解演習 ･････････････････････････････････････････････････････ *138*
- Part 6　Error Recognition／誤文訂正問題 ･････････････････････････････････････ *141*
- Part 7　Incomplete Sentence／文法・語彙問題 ･･･････････････････････････････ *143*

解　　答 ･･････････････････････････････････････････････････････････････････････････････ *144*

オンライン英語学習用テキスト
Linc English　GOLD Ⅰ

# Lesson 1 （http://audio.lincenglish.com にアクセスして音声を聞いてください）

## Part 1　Image Listening／写真描写問題

1. 左の写真を見て、人物の行動や物の位置などについて文を3つ作りなさい。
   _____
   _____
   _____

2. 写真の描写文として最も適切な文をA～Dの中から選びなさい。
   （A），（B），（C），（D）

1. 左の写真を見て、人物の行動や物の位置などについて文を3つ作りなさい。
   _____
   _____
   _____

2. 写真の描写文として最も適切な文をA～Dの中から選びなさい。
   （A），（B），（C），（D）

1. 左の写真を見て、人物の行動や物の位置などについて文を3つ作りなさい。
   _____
   _____
   _____

2. 写真の描写文として最も適切な文をA～Dの中から選びなさい。
   （A），（B），（C），（D）

1. 左の写真を見て、人物の行動や物の位置などについて文を3つ作りなさい。
   _____
   _____
   _____

2. 写真の描写文として最も適切な文をA～Dの中から選びなさい。
   （A），（B），（C），（D）

# Part 2　Question and Response／質疑応答問題

## 重要な質問表現

Do you know the height of Chicago's Sears Tower?
> height「高さ」をきかれている。

Are you an expert at dancing?
> expert「熟練者、専門家、プロ」。

Is the weather today suitable for a picnic?
> suitable for ～「～するのに適している」。

Why didn't you remind me to call him at noon?
> なぜ正午に彼に電話することを思い出させてくれなかったのですか？

Can you improve the organization of your essay?
> improve「改善する」。Organization「構造・組織・組み立て」。(A) I am positive は直訳「積極的です、確信しています」。

I would like to go with you to the concert.
> 質問文の come with me と相似しているのは (C) go with you であることから正解へと導ける。

Somehow I thought I had already met your brother.
> somehow「どういうわけか・なぜか」。

What did you do with the luggage?
> did you do with ～「～はどうしたのか・～に何があったのか」。

Do you plan to stay up to watch the baseball game on television?
> stay up「夜更かしをする」。

May I give you some advice?
> give advice「助言をする」。

## 確認ドリル

次の1～5の質問に対して最も適切な応答をそれぞれ (A)～(C) の中から選びなさい。

1. Would you consider a career as an author?
   - (A) No, I do not understand physics.
   - (B) To begin with, I do not have an automobile.
   - (C) No, I do not like to write.

2. Can you improve the organization of your essay?
   - (A) I am positive that I can make my essay better.
   - (B) I would like to read your essay.
   - (C) My essay is about primitive societies.

3. What would you do if you had a severe pain in your stomach?
   - (A) What a good idea!
   - (B) Maybe later.
   - (C) See a doctor.

4. Were you bored during the professor's lecture?
   - (A) I nearly fell asleep from lack of interest.
   - (B) Just call me tomorrow to arrange it.
   - (C) I'll listen to the lecture immediately.

5. Does he get along with his roommate?
   - (A) Yes, he plans to meet my roommate next week.
   - (B) Yes, he occasionally receives long email messages.
   - (C) Yes, he and his roommate rarely disagree.

## Part 3　Short Conversation／会話問題

次の会話を聞いて、質問に最も適当な答えを選びなさい。

### 質問文パターン

* What 型パターン

1. **A**：I'm so worried about my performance tonight. I have a major role in the dramatic production of *Romeo and Juliet*, and I just didn't get enough sleep last night.
   **B**：Oh, don't worry. I have confidence in you. You know your lines well, and you performed perfectly last night.
   **A**：Thanks for your praise, Julia. It's nearly time for the show to begin, and now I'm ready.

   **Q**：What does Julia mean when she says "I have confidence in you"?
   　　a. Scientific evidence says being tired does not affect a person's actions.
   　　b. I believe that you will perform well.
   　　c. I like the play *Romeo and Juliet*, and you have a good role.
   　　d. Last night's performance was excellent.

   解説：ジュリアが「あなたを信じています」と言ったのは、彼女の友達が perform well「上手に演技する」と信じていたから。

* How 型パターン

2. **A**：During spring vacation I went to the Yucatan Peninsula of Mexico. The best part of the trip was going to see the pyramids.
   **B**：I always thought that pyramids had been built only in Egypt.
   **A**：I used to think that too, but I realized that the Mayan people also built many pyramids. They were experts in mathematics. Without metal tools or even the wheel, they constructed cities in the jungle landscape with amazing architectural skill.

   **Q**：How were the Mayan people of Mexico able to construct pyramids?
   　　a. Mayans used metal tools and the wheel.
   　　b. Egyptians were the only people to build pyramids.
   　　c. Mayans were math experts and skilled builders.
   　　d. Egyptians taught the Mayans how to build pyramids.

   解説：メキシコのマヤ人たちは、experts in mathematics「数学の達人」であり amazing architectural skill「驚くべき建築技術」を用いてピラミッドを建設しました。

\* Why 型パターン

3. **A**：David, did you understand the teacher's explanation about Darwin's theory of evolution? I took careful notes and listened closely, but I'm still a little confused.
   **B**：Sorry, Peter. I wasn't paying attention. I was listening to music on my iPod.
   **A**：I can't help but think that you are going to have difficulty passing that course.

   **Q**：Why does Peter think David will do poorly in the course?
   a. He likes to pay attention to his teachers.
   b. He didn't listen to the explanation about evolution.
   c. He took notes but is still confused.
   d. He bought an iPod so he could listen to music.

   解説：デイビッドが悪い成績をとると思ったのは、彼が wasn't paying attention「ちゃんと聞いていなかった」からである。Can't help but で「～せざるを得ない」という意味。

\* How much 型パターン

4. **A**：I think I'll spend this weekend preparing for exams. I'll review English all day today and then work on American history and math tomorrow.
   **B**：Wouldn't you rather spend today playing tennis and then going out for dinner and a movie?
   **A**：Well, I guess I can manage to join you today and then study tomorrow.

   **Q**：How much time will be spent preparing for exams?
   a. Two days.　　b. One evening.
   c. One day.　　d. No time at all.

   解説：Study tomorrow「明日勉強する」ことになったので、試験の準備のために費やす時間は、1日である。

# Part 4　Short Talks ／説明文問題

次の説明文の質問に最も適当な答えを選びなさい。

### フォード社の歴史

In the early 1900's, automobiles were expensive, hand-made machines which only wealthy people could afford. In fact, a car factory was able to produce just a few of these luxury cars in a day. It was Henry Ford's dream to produce high-quality vehicles that were affordable to average Americans. His plan was to manufacture one model in large quantities. To accomplish this, Ford employed two strategies. One was to use interchangeable parts; the individual pieces for each car were identical. The other strategy he instituted at Ford Motor Company was to set up the assembly line. This meant that the car's parts were attached as the vehicle moved past workers, with each worker completing one specialized task. The Ford Model T was the first car that was mass produced using interchangeable parts. By 1914, the production of the Model T ran so smoothly that it took only 93 minutes to assemble one. The Model T was a commercial success, and by the time the Ford Company had manufactured 10 million cars, nine out of ten cars in the world were Fords.

1. What was one strategy Ford instituted to speed up car production?
   a. High-quality vehicles.　　b. Custom-made production.
   c. The assembly line.　　　d. Changing all of the parts.

2. Which was the first car to be mass produced using interchangeable parts?
   a. Henry Ford's dream car.　　b. Nine out of ten Fords.
   c. Mustang.　　　　　　　　　d. Model T.

解説：設問1　2つあった作戦のひとつが、同じ部品を使用する事で、もう1つが set up the assembly line「アセンブリーラインを設置」する事であった。正解1‐（C）

設問2　大量生産の第一号車は Model T であると文末できちんと説明されている。正解2‐（D）

### レナへの手紙

Dear Lena,

I hope you're enjoying your summer vacation as much as I am. I really like my job working as a server at a restaurant in Yellowstone National Park. Since the restaurant is a popular one, I'm working hard but making quite a lot in tips. I especially like talking with tourists from all over the world. Recently I served trout dinners to a cheerful Japanese family and buffalo burgers to three handsome men from France.

I have one day off a week and have been doing a lot of hiking. Last week a friend and I hitchhiked into Teton National Park, south of here, and hiked into Jenny Lake, a beautiful alpine area. We saw mountain goats on the trail and found huge meadows blanketed with wildflowers. We'll do an 18-mile hike next time.

It's hard to believe that school starts in three weeks. I'll see you soon!

Your friend,

Michelle

1. What is Michelle's job?
   a. Tour guide.     b. Wildlife expert.
   c. Waitress.      d. Restaurant owner.

2. Which activity is Michelle's favorite during her time off from work?
   a. Hiking.        b. Swimming.
   c. Photography.   d. Cooking.

解説：設問1　レストランで as a server「料理を出す人」として働き、tips「チップ」ももらえていることからウェイトレスと判断する。正解－(C)

設問2　休みの日には、have been doing a lot of hiking「ハイキングをたくさんしている」というところから、彼女がハイキングを好んでいることがわかる。正解－(A)

# Part 5　Reading／読解演習

次の段落文を読み、各設問に対して最も適切な答えを選びなさい（各段落速読問題は2分以内に終わらせなさい）。

### スピードリーディング

　Today is the first day of the University of Montana's spring semester. The spring semester is the second half of the academic year. Although it is called the spring semester, the thirteen-week stretch of school actually begins in the winter, near the end of January. By contrast, the academic year begins with the autumn semester. The autumn semester actually begins in late summer, usually at the end of August, and continues until the end of the calendar year. All students take a break from late December through early January.

　　1. In which season is the month of January?
　　　　a. Winter.　　　b. Spring.
　　　　c. Summer.　　　d. Autumn.

　　2. What is the first semester of the academic year called?
　　　　a. Winter semester.　　　b. Spring semester.
　　　　c. Summer semester.　　　d. Autumn semester.

　This discrepancy between the academic and calendar years is caused by America's agricultural history. Children needed to spend the summer months working on family farms, and so school ended at the beginning of the growing season and began again near harvest time. Although the beginning of the academic year is a time of new experiences and sensations for students, it comes just as the natural world is settling into a winter slumber. By contrast, the beginning of the spring semester comes in the depths of winter but catches students just as they are beginning to blossom as students.

　　1. What activity was school originally scheduled to allow children to participate in?
　　　　a. Camp.　　　b. Vacations.
　　　　c. Farming.　　d. Tourism.

　　2. To what activity does the author compare nature during winter?
　　　　a. Walking.　　b. Sleeping.
　　　　c. Talking.　　d. Tanning.

　The beginning of the spring semester feels different than the beginning of the academic year. At the start of the autumn semester, first-year students—called frosh—are new to campus and unfamiliar with the location of buildings, essential services and most of the people around them. The students are visibly anxious and tentative in their new surroundings. There may be a few new things for frosh to deal with at the beginning of the spring semester, but the campus and its people are largely familiar even to first-year students.

8

1. Someone observing behavior on the first day of the spring semester would notice _____ the autumn semester.
   a. a passage from.        b. an amenity to.
   c. a difference from.     d. hostility to.

2. How should first-year students feel by the beginning of the spring semester?
   a. Identified.     b. Acclimatized.
   c. Bound.          d. Welcome.

スピードリーディングで読んだものと同じ文を読みます。各設問に対して最も適切な答えを選びなさい。

読解問題

Today is the first day of the University of Montana's spring semester. The spring semester is the second half of the academic year. Although it is called the spring semester, the thirteen-week stretch of school actually begins in the winter, near the end of January. By contrast, the academic year begins with the autumn semester. The autumn semester actually begins in late summer, usually at the end of August, and continues until the end of the calendar year. All students take a break from late December through early January.

This discrepancy between the academic and calendar years is caused by America's agricultural history. Children needed to spend the summer months working on family farms, and so school ended at the beginning of the growing season and began again near harvest time. Although the beginning of the academic year is a time of new experiences and sensations for students, it comes just as the natural world is settling into a winter slumber. By contrast, the beginning of the spring semester comes in the depths of winter but catches students just as they are beginning to blossom as students.

The beginning of the spring semester feels different than the beginning of the academic year. At the start of the autumn semester, first-year students—called frosh—are new to campus and unfamiliar with the location of buildings, essential services and most of the people around them. The students are visibly anxious and tentative in their new surroundings. There may be a few new things for frosh to deal with at the beginning of the spring semester, but the campus and its people are largely familiar even to first-year students.

The comfort of first-year students shows itself in the way these students carry themselves. In class discussions, they are less tentative and more forthcoming. In the hallways, they shout greetings to friends instead of hunting with their eyes for any familiar faces. Many are returning to boyfriends or girlfriends who have been far away for a long time. So while the spring semester is a new beginning, it comes without the awkwardness of first starts.

Comprehension Questions

1. What are the sections of the academic year at the University of Montana called?
   a. Annuals.     b. Semesters.
   c. Quarters.    d. Seasons.

Answer: b

2. During which season do students mostly not go to school?
   a. Winter.     b. Spring.
   c. Summer.     d. Autumn.

3. What difference between the autumn and spring semesters does the author highlight?
   a. The weather.               b. The experiences of frosh.
   c. The material covered in classes.   d. The cost of attending.

4. How does the author describe first starts?
   a. Inconsistent.     b. Unreliable.
   c. Uncomfortable.    d. Incapable.

# Part 6　Error Recognition／誤文訂正問題

各文には文法的な誤りがあります。訂正もしくは書き換えを必要とする語や語句を選びなさい。

1. I've <u>tried</u> every <u>trick</u> I can <u>thinks</u> of, and I <u>still</u> can't fall asleep easily.
   　　　 A　　　　　　 B　　　　　 C　　　　　　　 D

   解説：can「〜できる」の後にはいつも原形動詞が続くので thinks を think に直す必要がある。

   正しい英文：I've tried every trick I can think of, and I still can't fall asleep easily.

2. <u>Unfortunately</u>, Carrie's <u>ambition</u> <u>to sang</u> professionally is not <u>matched</u> by her talent.
   　　 A　　　　　　　　　 B　　　　 C　　　　　　　　　　　　　 D

   解説：to に動詞が続く場合は不定詞になり、動詞が原形でなければならない。よって、過去形の sang を原形の sing に直す必要がある。

   正しい英文：Unfortunately, Carrie's ambition to sing professionally is not matched by her talent.

3. "Please, you don't have to <u>yelling</u> at me. I'm <u>standing</u> right <u>here</u> and can <u>hear</u> you perfectly well, "Kathy stated.
   　　　　　　　　　　　　 A　　　　　　　 B　　　　 C　　　　　 D

   解説：to に動詞が続く場合は不定詞になり、動詞が原形でなければならない。よって、現在分詞の yelling を原形の yell に直す必要がある。

   正しい英文："Please, you don't have to yell at me. I'm standing right here and can hear you perfectly well," Kathy stated.

4. The <u>latest</u> showing of the movie <u>should</u> get out <u>above</u> midnight. Would that be too <u>late</u> for your
   　　 A　　　　　　　　　　　　 B　　　　　　 C　　　　　　　　　　　　　　　 D
   babysitter?

   解説：前置詞 above は「〜の上の」という位置を示す語で、「深夜」という言葉とはかみ合わない。「深夜ごろ」の意味になる前置詞 about が最も適当。

   正しい英文：The latest showing of the movie should get out about midnight. Would that be too late for your babysitter?

5. I was <u>unable</u> to get an <u>opinions</u> on the matter. I'm still not sure if it is an <u>inherited</u> or a learned <u>trait</u>.
   　　　　 A　　　　　　 B　　　　　　　　　　　　　　　　　　　　　　　 C　　　　　　　　　 D

   解説：冠詞 an「ひとつの」に続くので、名詞も単数形に直す。

   正しい英文：I was unable to get an opinion on the matter. I'm still not sure if it is an inherited or a learned trait.

6. The <u>new</u> swimming <u>facility</u> will open its doors in June and will be <u>available</u> to our team for <u>regularly</u>
   　　　 A　　　　　　 B　　　　　　　　　　　　　　　　　　　　　 C　　　　　　　　　　　 D
   practice.

   解説：副詞は動詞・形容詞を修飾し、形容詞は名詞を修飾する。practice は名詞なので、修飾語は形容詞でないといけない。よって、regularly を regular に直す。

正しい英文：The new swimming facility will open its doors in June and will be available to our team for regular practice.

7. I was <u>pleased</u> and touched to see the youngster <u>expressed</u> <u>such</u> sweet <u>affection</u> for his new sister.
   A            B  C    D

解説：to ＋ see ＋人＋原形動詞「(人) が (動詞) するのを見る」という言い回し。よって expressed は原形の express でないといけない。

正しい英文：I was pleased and touched to see the youngster express such sweet affection for his new sister.

# Part 7　Incomplete Sentence／文法・語彙問題

文法的に適切な語や語句を1つ選び、文を完成させなさい。

1. David _____ my presence by nodding his head and smiling at me.
    a. to acknowledge　　b. acknowledged
    c. acknowledging　　d. is acknowledged

   訳：デイビッドは笑顔でうなずいて私が居ることを確認した。
   解説：文中に動詞がないことからまずAとCではないことがわかる。またデイビッドが出席を確認している本人ということから受動態であるとは考えにくいよってBのacknowledgedが正解である。

2. A _____ problem with the aircraft caused our flight to be delayed and caused me a great deal of anxiety about boarding the plane again.
    a. having mechanical　　b. mechanic
    c. having mechanic　　d. mechanical

   訳：飛行機の故障のために、私はフライトが遅れることと再び飛行機に乗る怖さを思い出してしまった。
   解説：冠詞Aと名詞problemの間にあることから下線部が名詞を修飾する形容詞であることがわかる。よって正解はD。

3. The crow swooped down onto the lawn and the robins _____ upwards into the tree branches.
    a. scattering　　b. scatters
    c. scattered　　d. to be scattered

   訳：カラスが芝生へ急降下し、コマドリが木立へと飛び立った。
   解説：カラスのswooped「襲い掛かった」に対比してコマドリの文が続くので、カラスと同じ過去形動詞でなければならない。よってCのscattered「四散した」が正解。

4. _____ mercury were found at levels high enough to warrant an immediate investigation by the Food and Drug Administration.
    a. Traced　　b. To trace
    c. Traces of　　d. Traceable

   訳：FDAによる早急な検査を依頼するのに十分な高濃度の水銀の痕跡が検知された。
   解説：mercuryが主語に当たるので、Bの不定詞副詞用法「水銀を追跡するため」はおかしい。AもDも文法的はおかしくないが、意味から考えるとCがもっとも適当。

5. I'm not _____ keen on seeing that movie. Let's plan on dinner instead.
    a. as to　　b. something
    c. some　　d. very

   訳：私はそれほどその映画を見たいと思っていないので、代わりにディナーを計画しましょう。
   解説：keenは形容詞で、それを修飾できるのは副詞だけなので、Dが正解。

# Lesson 2 （http://audio.lincenglish.com にアクセスして音声を聞いてください）

## Part 1　Image Listening／写真描写問題

1. 左の写真を見て、人物の行動や物の位置などについて文を3つ作りなさい。
   _____
   _____
   _____

2. 写真の描写文として最も適切な文をA～Dの中から選びなさい。
   （A），（B），（C），（D）

1. 左の写真を見て、人物の行動や物の位置などについて文を3つ作りなさい。
   _____
   _____
   _____

2. 写真の描写文として最も適切な文をA～Dの中から選びなさい。
   （A），（B），（C），（D）

1. 左の写真を見て、人物の行動や物の位置などについて文を3つ作りなさい。
   _____
   _____
   _____

2. 写真の描写文として最も適切な文をA～Dの中から選びなさい。
   （A），（B），（C），（D）

1. 左の写真を見て、人物の行動や物の位置などについて文を3つ作りなさい。
   _____
   _____
   _____

2. 写真の描写文として最も適切な文をA～Dの中から選びなさい。
   （A），（B），（C），（D）

# Part 2  Question and Response／質疑応答問題

## 重要な質問表現

Is that the former president?
　　former「以前の・前者の」の類義語は previous, past などが挙げられる。

Has fuel gotten more expensive again?
　　fuel は車のガソリンなどの「燃料」のこと。

Do you ever just stare into space?
　　stare into space とはつまり、ぼーっと一点を見つめて静止している状態を示す。

Would you want to be an astronaut?
　　astronaut「宇宙飛行士」も、一つの職業の名称として覚えておこう。

It is a spectacular sight.
　　spectacular「壮観な」。

Who is in charge?
　　be in charge「係りの、〜担当の」。

Why did she become the group's president?
　　president は「大統領」というのが一般的だが、小さなグループやサークルなどの「リーダー」、あるいは「長」としても用いられる。

Which shift do you work?
　　時間や曜日によって働く時間が決められているのが shift「交代制」である。

How would you like your steak done?
　　ステーキの焼き具合をリクエストするときに使える表現。Well-done「完全に焼く」、medium「中くらい」、rare「生焼け」となる。

Did you hear the distant thunder?
　　thunder「雷」は嵐がもうじき来る、あるいは来ている証拠。

## 確認ドリル

次の1〜5の質問に対して最も適切な応答をそれぞれ（A）〜（C）の中から選びなさい。

1. Why does he always complain about his job?
   (A)　Well, he often works extra hours.
   (B)　He is happy with his work.
   (C)　He is looking for something new.

2. Did he make the basket?
   (A)　Yes, with a lucky shot.
   (B)　Next time I go first.
   (C)　We'll play 18 holes.

3. Why did she become a teacher?
   (A)　Because she must try harder.
   (B)　Because she wanted to educate children.
   (C)　Because the book was easy for her to read.

4. Why doesn't she like him?
   (A)　Because he acts superior to everyone.
   (B)　Because the other car is better.
   (C)　Because they will go to Europe soon.

5. How does the song make you feel?
   (A)　I sing it often.
   (B)　I'm filled with joy.
   (C)　I heard it yesterday.

# Part 3　Short Conversation ／会話問題

次の会話を聞いて、質問に最も適当な答えを選びなさい。

### 質問文パターン

* Which 型パターン

1. **A**：I think it's interesting that television stations broadcast debates between political candidates. Did you watch the debate last night, Sue?
   **B**：Yes, I did. I thought Mr. Alexander was definitely inferior to Mr. Bennett.
   **A**：That was my opinion, too.

   **Q**：Which candidate did Sue favor in the debate?
   　　a. Mr. Alexander.　　b. Neither.
   　　c. Mr. Bennett.　　d. Unknown.

   解説：していた候補者は、Mr. Bennett「ベネット氏」である。

* How 型パターン

2. **A**：The effort of some athletes really inspires me. For example, Lance Armstrong had cancer and then trained so thoroughly that he was able to win the Tour de France bicycle race several times.
   **B**：So, Tucker, what are you going to do to become more physically fit?
   **A**：I'll try jogging. I'd also like to begin bicycling long distances, although I don't want to race.

   **Q**：How has Tucker become inspired by Lance Armstrong?
   　　a. He plans to participate in bicycle　　b. He will overcome cancer.
   　　　racing and jogging.
   　　c. He plans to become more fit by joggin　　d. He will compete in the Tour de France.
   　　　and bicycling.

   解説：アームストロングによって触発されたタッカーさんは、try jogging「ジョギングに挑戦する」つもりである。また、bicycling long distances「長距離のサイクリング」も始めたいと思っている。

* Why 型パターン

3. **A**：If you're driving to the theater, I would advise you to avoid University Avenue. There's a traffic jam in front of the science building.
   **B**：What's causing the traffic problem?
   **A**：Two big trucks are parked near the construction site of the new museum. They're blocking the road because the drivers are delivering building materials.

**Q**：Why are the trucks blocking the road and causing a traffic jam?

  a. Because they're parkednear the theater.
  b. Because drivers are carrying science equipment.
  c. Because drivers are delivering construction materials
  d. Because they're opening a new museum.

解説：そのトラックが道路を塞いで交通渋滞を引き起こしているのは、because the drivers are delivering building materials「そのトラックの運転手たちが建築資材を運び入れているため」である。

\* What 型パターン

4. **A**：In this morning's newspaper I read a letter to the editor stating that garbage thrown in the local river is poisoning the fish.
   **B**：What did the writer suggest?
   **A**：She concluded her letter by begging readers to meet on Saturday to help clean up the river. I think I'll join the effort.

**Q**：What did the writer of the letter to the editor request?

  a. Garbage is poisoning fish.
  b. People are throwing garbage in the river.
  c. Readers need to help clean up the river.
  d. Newspaper is poisoning fish.

解説：筆者は、begging readers to meet on Saturday to help clean up the river「川をきれいにするために、土曜日に会うことを読者に求め」ていた。

## Part 4　Short Talks／説明文問題

次の説明文の質問に最も適当な答えを選びなさい。

### 健康問題

You've heard the warning: If you're going to be in the sun, apply sunscreen. What is that creamy substance many of us slather on our skin? Sunscreen is a combination of organic and inorganic ingredients. The inorganic ingredients like zinc oxide reflect or scatter the ultraviolet (UV) radiation, while organic ingredients absorb the UV radiation, dissipating it as heat. It is the UV rays that cause sunburn and harmful effects such as skin cancer.

When purchasing sunscreen, the Sun Protection Factor, or SPF, measures how effectively the sunscreen formula limits skin exposure to UV-B rays that burn the skin. The higher the SPF, the more protection the sunscreen will provide against UV-B rays. While sunscreen doesn't prevent harm from the sun's rays, it can offer some protection. With the death rate from skin cancer in the U.S. increasing about 4% a year since 1973, using sunscreen definitely makes sense.

1. What is the job of the inorganic ingredients in sunscreen?
   a. To create a soothing cream.
   b. To cause sunburns and harmful effects.
   c. To reflect the ultraviolet radiation.
   d. To heat the ultraviolet radiation.

2. Which of these would be the most effective sunscreen formula?
   a. UV-B.
   b. SPF 10.
   c. UV of 4%.
   d. SPF 50.

解説：設問1　日焼け止めだからこそ、皮膚を守る効能でないとおかしい。よって（C）がこの場合もっとも正しい答えとなる。正解－（C）

設問2　本文には The higher the SPF, the more protection the sunscreen will provide against UV-B rays「SPFの数値が高いほど、紫外線を防ぐ率が高い」とあるので、（D）の50が正しい。正解－（D）

### シカゴのホットドッグ

If you visit Chicago, Illinois, try a Chicago-style hot dog. This tasty food was popular during the Great Depression when money was scarce and a hot dog provided a hot meal on a bun for only a nickel. Today the price is higher, but a Chicago-style hot dog is still a full-sized meal. The main ingredient is a boiled all-beef hot dog. The dog is placed on a steamed poppy seed bun. Adding the traditional toppings is sometimes labeled "dragging (or walking) the dog through the garden" because of the vegetables that are included. First, sprinkle on tangy pickle relish and raw chopped white onion. Then, place two tomato wedges on the bun and add a little celery salt. Finally, apply yellow mustard to the hot dog in a decorative zigzag fashion. Cucumber slices or a dill pickle spear can be substituted for the pickle relish, but ketchup must never be used. The hot dog is ready to be enjoyed, Chicago-style.

1. What type of bun is required for a Chicago-style hot dog?
    a. Whole wheat.　　b. Poppy seed.
    c. Extra large.　　d. Toasted.

2. Which ingredient should never be used on a Chicago-style hot dog?
    a. Mustard.　　　　　　b. Dill pickle.
    c. Chopped white onion.　　d. Ketchup.

解説：設問1　本文ではシカゴスタイル用のバンは steamed poppy seed bun「蒸して温められた、ポピーシード入りのパン」とあるので、(B) が正解となる。正解－(B)

設問2　最後から2文目を参照。マスタードと刻み玉ねぎは本文からして必要不可欠であり、ディルピクルスは can be substituted「代用して」もよいとのことなので、消去法でもやはり (D) が正解となる。正解－(D)

# Part 5　Reading／読解演習

次の段落文を読み、各設問に対して最も適切な答えを選びなさい（各段落速読問題は 2 分以内に終わらせなさい）。

**スピードリーディング**

　John's first job after college was as an investment banker. When he was in high school, he imagined being an investment banker. At the time, John never learned what an investment banker did or how he should go about getting hired as one. John saw the occupation listed on the information sheet of a patient at the doctor's office where he did some filing. He liked the way that the title sounded.

　1. Which of the following jobs did John have when he was in high school?
　　　a. Clerk.　　　b. Counselor.
　　　c. Waiter.　　 d. Investment banker.

　2. What did John like about investment banking when he first learned about it?
　　　a. The people he would be working with.　　b. The preparation it would take to get employed.
　　　c. The work he would be doing.　　d. The way the job title sounded.

　John forgot about being interested in investment banking when he went off to college. His interest in studying human nature, however, brought him into a class where economics was being taught. Money motivates so much about the choices people make in life; it seemed that he would need to study the theory of the stuff in order to understand other humans. The teacher was someone special, one of the rare and truly gifted communicators who can make a subject come alive. John decided to study economics.

　1. What was John's main interest when he was at college?
　　　a. Recreation.　　　b. Investment banking.
　　　c. Human nature.　　d. Theory.

　2. Why did John first decide to take an economics class?
　　　a. Because he wanted to become an investment banker.　　b. Because it fulfilled a requirement.
　　　c. Because of the importance of money.　　d. Because he heard it was easy.

　And John excelled in his studies, which also included philosophy as a major subject. In combination, philosophy and economics gave John a view into human nature. Philosophy taught him the ageless controversies of human understanding and the answers to those questions that have been proposed since antiquity. Economics supplied analytical tools that he could turn toward supplying his own answers. By chance more than anything else, John even took a course in corporate finance during his last semester of college. He never imagined that he would put it to use so soon afterward.

1. What did John find useful about economics?
    a. Preparing for corporate finance.   b. Learning how to analyze things.
    c. Becoming considerate.              d. Measuring capital flows.

2. Why did John take a corporate finance class?
    a. Because he knew it would be useful.      b. Because he happened to take theclass by chance.
    c. Because he thought it would be enjoyable. d. Because he respected the teacher.

スピードリーディングで読んだものと同じ文を読みます。各設問に対して最も適切な答えを選びなさい。

**読解問題**

John's first job after college was as an investment banker. When he was in high school, he imagined being an investment banker. At the time, John never learned what an investment banker did or how he should go about getting hired as one. John saw the occupation listed on the information sheet of a patient at the doctor's office where he did some filing. He liked the way that the title sounded.

John forgot about being interested in investment banking when he went off to college. His interest in studying human nature, however, brought him into a class where economics was being taught. Money motivates so much about the choices people make in life; it seemed that he would need to study the theory of the stuff in order to understand other humans. The teacher was someone special, one of the rare and truly gifted communicators who can make a subject come alive. John decided to study economics.

And John excelled in his studies, which also included philosophy as a major subject. In combination, philosophy and economics gave John a view into human nature. Philosophy taught him the ageless controversies of human understanding and the answers to those questions that have been proposed since antiquity. Economics supplied analytical tools that he could turn toward supplying his own answers. By chance more than anything else, John even took a course in corporate finance during his last semester of college. He never imagined that he would put it to use so soon afterward.

But graduation came and went, and John stayed in the small Indiana town where his college was located. He split his time between hiking in the outdoors and reading books from the campus library, where John retained his full borrowing privileges. But John's money was running out. The only job in the town where he was living was in a factory. John thought he would have to take it, at least temporarily, in order to sustain himself. Instead, just weeks later, he had a job in one of New York City's tallest buildings. The events that brought him there were unexpected but, remembering his fascination with the title of investment banker, perhaps they could have been anticipated.

Comprehension Questions

1. How soon after college did John become an investment banker?
    a. Immediately.     b. Not long after.
    c. Years later.     d. Never.

2. What subject did John supplement his economics education with?
    a. Mathematics.     b. Computer science.
    c. Philosophy.      d. Psychology.

3. What does the author imply about John working in a factory?
    a. John worked in a factory and liked it.
    b. John never worked in a factory but would have liked it.
    c. John never worked in a factory and would not have liked it.
    d. John worked in a factory and did not like it.

4. What does the author imply about John's job as an investment banker?
    a. He would not like it.
    b. He never deserved it.
    c. He got it by chance.
    d. He had been working for it his whole life.

## Part 6  Error Recognition／誤文訂正問題

各文には文法的な誤りがあります。訂正もしくは書き換えを必要とする語や語句を選びなさい。

1. There <u>really</u> isn't a <u>tricked</u> to opening this container. <u>Just</u> lift up <u>on</u> the lid.
   　　　　A　　　　　　B　　　　　　　　　　　　　　　C　　　　　　D

   解説：冠詞のaの後には名詞が来なければならないのに、過去分詞が続いているので、trickedを名詞のtrickに直す。

   正しい英文：There really isn't a trick to opening this container. Just lift up on the lid.

2. Their <u>argument</u> was <u>about</u> <u>whether</u> or not the platypus is a <u>mammals</u>.
   　　　　A　　　　　　B　　　C　　　　　　　　　　　　　　　　D

   解説：冠詞aが単数を示しているのに、続く名詞がmammalsと複数形になっているので、単数形に直す。

   正しい英文：Their argument was about whether or not the platypus is a mammal.

3. The <u>visual</u> team in the J.C. Penney <u>store</u> was <u>responsibility</u> for creating <u>appealing</u> and efficient shopping areas.
   　　　A　　　　　　　　　　　　　　　B　　　　　　C　　　　　　　　　　　D

   解説：be responsible for で「〜の責任がある」と言う熟語なので、responsibility を responsible に直す。

   正しい英文：The visual team in the J.C. Penney store was responsible for creating appealing and efficient shopping areas.

4. The <u>dispute</u> will not be resolved if we continue <u>arguing</u> these issues. I believe we need <u>looking</u> beyond the
   　　　A　　　　　　　　　　　　　　　　　　　　B　　　　　　　　　　　　　　　　　　　　C
   opinions we've <u>held</u> for so long.
   　　　　　　　D

   解説：need は不定詞をとるが動名詞はとらない。よって need looking はとても不自然。need looking を need to look に直す。

   正しい英文：The dispute will not be resolved if we continue arguing these issues. I believe we need to look beyond the opinions we've held for so long.

5. I <u>watched</u> as the workers <u>peeled</u> strip after strip of shingles <u>from</u> the old roof. Who would have <u>suspecting</u>
   　　A　　　　　　　　　　　B　　　　　　　　　　　　　　　　　　C　　　　　　　　　　　　　　　　D
   there were so many layers?

   解説：完了形を示す have の後に現在分詞の suspecting が続いている。完了形は have (has)＋過去分詞 なので、suspecting を過去分詞の suspected に直す。

   正しい英文：I watched as the workers peeled strip after strip of shingles from the old roof. Who would have suspected there were so many layers?

6. No, underage drinking is not <u>inevitable</u>. It is <u>upped</u> to parents and <u>other</u> adults to provide <u>direction</u> and
   　　　　　　　　　　　　　　　　A　　　　　　　　B　　　　　　　　　C　　　　　　　　　　D
   example to our youth.

解説：be + up to で「〜次第である」という熟語。よって upped を up に直す。

正しい英文：No, underage drinking is not inevitable. It is up to parents and other adults to provide direction and example to our youth.

7. I don't <u>know</u> about you, but I <u>think</u> that tale is an urban <u>myth</u>; at least I <u>certain</u> hope so.
    A       B        C     D

解説：主語代名詞 I と動詞の間に名詞が来るのが不自然。修飾できる語が動詞しかないので、副詞形の certainly に変えることで意味が成り立つ。

正しい英文：I don't know about you, but I think that tale is an urban myth; at least I certainly hope so.

# Part 7   Incomplete Sentence／文法・語彙問題

文法的に適切な語や語句を1つ選び、文を完成させなさい。

1. There was a decided lack of enthusiasm in the group when we _____ that it was our turn to clean the bathrooms.
    a. were telling    b. am told
    c. were told       d. tells

   訳：私たちのがトイレ掃除の当番だと言われた時、明らかに私たちのグループはやる気に欠けていた。
   解説：BとDは主語weから考えて明らかに不適当。残りAもCもともに文法的におかしくないが、意味合いから考えてCが最も適当。(decidedの意味は「決心した」ではなく「明らかに」)。

2. There is a definite lack of _____ in our nation among those with money and those without.
    a. equal           b. being equality
    c. is equal        d. equality

   訳：わが国における財産を持つ者と持たない者の差は明らかに不平等だ。
   解説：lack of（名詞）で「〜の不足」。選択肢の中で名詞はDのみ。

3. My little sister had _____ down at the grocery store.  Mother wouldn't buy her chocolate chips.
    a. melting         b. melt
    c. a melted        d. a melt

   訳：妹がスーパーマーケットでだだをこねた。お母さんがチョコレートを買ってあげないと言っていたからだ。
   解説：melt downはそのまま直訳すると「溶けてしまう」だが、「駄々をこねる」とも訳される。melt downは可算名詞なのでDが正解。

4. I'm _____ awake, and you expect me to help you make plans for a trip to the lake?
    a. bare            b. barely
    c. bared           d. so baring

   訳：まだ起きたばかりだというのに、湖への旅行のプランを作るのを手伝えと言うのですか？
   解説：「起きている」という形容詞を修飾する語でないといけないので、副詞のAが最も適当。barelyは「わずかに、かろうじて」という意味。

5. It is infrequent that we see _____ gems. Most, I believe, are created in the lab using extreme temperatures.
    a. genuinely       b. be genuine
    c. genuine         d. become genuin

   訳：純粋な宝石を目にすることができるのは稀である。私の知る限り、ほとんどの宝石は製造所で高熱加工されたものである。
   解説：seeの目的語のgemsを修飾できるのは形容詞のみなのでCのgenuineが正解。

# Lesson 3 （http://audio.lincenglish.com にアクセスして音声を聞いてください）

## Part 1　Image Listening／写真描写問題

1. 左の写真を見て、人物の行動や物の位置などについて文を3つ作りなさい。
   _____
   _____
   _____

2. 写真の描写文として最も適切な文をA～Dの中から選びなさい。
   (A), (B), (C), (D)

1. 左の写真を見て、人物の行動や物の位置などについて文を3つ作りなさい。
   _____
   _____
   _____

2. 写真の描写文として最も適切な文をA～Dの中から選びなさい。
   (A), (B), (C), (D)

1. 左の写真を見て、人物の行動や物の位置などについて文を3つ作りなさい。
   _____
   _____
   _____

2. 写真の描写文として最も適切な文をA～Dの中から選びなさい。
   (A), (B), (C), (D)

1. 左の写真を見て、人物の行動や物の位置などについて文を3つ作りなさい。
   _____
   _____
   _____

2. 写真の描写文として最も適切な文をA～Dの中から選びなさい。
   (A), (B), (C), (D)

# Part 2　Question and Response ／質疑応答問題

## 重要な質問表現

When will the chicks emerge from the eggs?

　　　卵からかえる実質期間をきかれている。emerge「（ひなが卵から）かえる」。

I perceive a problem.

　　　perceive「気づく」。

Yes, they came to an agreement.

　　　2人の仲を気にしている様子から、喧嘩でもしていたのだろうか。

Where did that new TV screen come from?

　　　そのテレビがどこで製造されたものか。

Will the movie star make an appearance?

　　　make an appearance「姿を現す」。

He wants to convince them he is right.

　　　convince「納得させる・確信させる」。

I heard she had a clever solution.

　　　clever「賢い」は人の性格を述べる場合にも使うことができる。

After I find an alternative.

　　　alternative「代わるもの・代案」。

Do you plan to purchase all of your gifts on-line?

　　　on line「インターネット上で」。

It is worth more than I'll ever earn.

　　　worth「価値がある」。

## 確認ドリル

次の1〜5の質問に対して最も適切な応答をそれぞれ（A）〜（C）の中から選びなさい。

1. Why are they cheering?
   - （A）Because they lost the game.
   - （B）Because they defeated the other team.
   - （C）Because the noise is loud.

2. Do you think you'll get your stolen purse back?
   - （A）The last time I checked it wasn't there.
   - （B）I hope so as I'm offering a reward.
   - （C）It had fifty dollars in it.

3. Do you know why they are having a conflict?
   - （A）He wants to eat pizza.
   - （B）They both like the same girl.
   - （C）The car won't start.

4. How did they know one another?
   - （A）She is very nervous.
   - （B）She is his employee.
   - （C）She always talks on her cell phone.

5. Why did they turn their backs on her?
   - （A）Because they are trying to ignore her.
   - （B）Because she is trying to get their attention.
   - （C）Because they want to support her ideas.

# Part 3　Short Conversation／会話問題

次の会話を聞いて、質問に最も適当な答えを選びなさい。

### 質問文パターン

＊ Why 型パターン

1. **A**：Do you know anything about your ancestors?
   **B**：My father's father left northern Italy and moved to the United States at the end of the 1800's. My father's mother was born in England, but she traveled to Panama to help nurse the builders of the Panama Canal who became ill from diseases carried by insects. She met my grandfather in Seattle.
   **A**：What a story! I'd like to hear more about their experiences.

   **Q**：Why was the grandmother in Panama?
   　　a. To study diseases carried by insects.　　b. To go to northern Italy.
   　　c. To help build the Panama Canal.　　d. To nurse sick workers.

   解説：祖母がパナマにいたのは、to help nurse the builders of the Panama Canal「パナマ運河を建設していた人々を看護するため」でした。

＊ What 型パターン

2. **A**：I've been reading about the ship called the *Titanic*. It was sailing from England to the United States. It hit an iceberg which caused it to sink.
   **B**：Many of the passengers on the *Titanic* died. Those that fell into the water did not last long because the ocean water is so cold. Also, there weren't enough life boats, so some people just went down with the ship.
   **A**：The *Titanic* was called the ship that couldn't sink. Someone was obviously wrong.

   **Q**：What caused the *Titanic* to sink?
   　　a. Ocean water is so cold.　　b. Many passengers died.
   　　c. Hit an iceberg.　　d. Not enough life boats.

   解説：タイタニック号は、hit an iceberg which caused it to sink「氷山にぶつかり、それが原因で沈没しました」。

＊ Where 型パターン

3. **A**：I'm looking for the trail that leads to the lake.
   **B**：Let me guide you. I know where that trail begins.
   **A**：Thanks. I'm anxious to go for a swim.

   **Q**：Where does the trail go?
   　　a. To the guide.　　b. The beginning.
   　　c. For a swim.　　d. To the lake.

解説：その道は、the trail that leads to the lake「湖に続く道」です。

* Who 型パターン

4. **A**：Did you ever meet my former roommate?

   **B**：Yes, Lee, you introduced her to me several weeks ago at the party given by your current roommate.

   **A**：She's just become engaged to be married. I don't oppose her marriage to William, but I hope she isn't rushing into it.

   **Q**：Who is engaged to be married?
   - a. Former roommate.
   - b. Lee.
   - c. New roommate.
   - d. Current roommate.

   解説：婚約したのは、前のルームメイトである。rush into で「あせって〜する」という意味。

## Part 4  Short Talks／説明文問題

次の説明文の質問に最も適当な答えを選びなさい。

### テーブルマナー

Table manners refer to polite behaviors while eating at the table. Table manners are different in different cultures. For example, in Japan it is considered normal to make a slurping sound when eating noodles. This would be considered rude in some countries, such as the United States. In China, it is rude to eat everything on your plate. In Saudi Arabia, people can eat with their hand, as long as it is the right hand only. In France, if you ask for ketchup, the cook will think you don't like the food. Finally, the Inuit people in Canada burp to show the cook that they like the food. This would be considered rude in many other cultures. So you see, it is important to learn about table manners before you travel!

1. What did the paragraph say about Chinese table manners?
   a. You must burp if you like the food.
   b. The cook will not eat with the others.
   c. It is impolite to finish all of the food on your plate.
   d. You must eat with your left hand only.

2. What will a French cook think if you ask for ketchup?
   a. That you don't like the food.
   b. That you are an American.
   c. That you are still hungry.
   d. That you love tomatoes.

解説：設問1　rude to eat everything on your plate「食べきってしまうのは失礼」と本文にあるので、(C) が正解。正解−(C)

設問2　the cook will think you don't like the food「あなたは出された料理が気に入らなかったとコックは思う」とある。よって正解には (A) を選ぶ。正解−(A)

### ジュピター

Jupiter is the largest planet in our solar system. Its mass is 317 times more than Earth. Jupiter has 28 moons and a large red spot that is visible with a powerful telescope. This red spot is actually a huge storm like a hurricane that covers an area bigger than Earth. Scientists think that this storm has been active for at least 300 years. There is no solid surface on Jupiter. In other words, the sky gradually becomes the ocean; there is nothing in between. Jupiter spins very quickly, and it only takes about ten hours to go from day to night. Because of this, the shape of Jupiter is short and wide.

1. What is the red spot seen on Jupiter?
   a. It is a reflection of Earth's water.
   b. It is one of Jupiter's moons.
   c. It is a large ocean.
   d. It is a huge hurricane-like storm.

2. Why is Jupiter short and wide?
   a. Because it spins so quickly.  b. Because the temperature is so hot.
   c. Because its moons often hit it.  d. Because of the hurricane.

解説：設問1　地球よりも大きいサイズの a huge storm like a hurricane「ハリーケーン似た嵐」のようなものと本文にあるので、(D) が正解。正解－(D)

設問2　自転の速度が早いために、遠心力で天体が横長に伸びるのが原因なので、(A) が正解。正解－(A)

# Part 5  Reading ／読解演習

次の段落文を読み、各設問に対して最も適切な答えを選びなさい（各段落速読問題は 2 分以内に終わらせなさい）。

### スピードリーディング

John had never been to New York City before his interview to be an investment banker. It was the first job interview he had after graduating from college, his first attempt to translate his education into an occupation. John stumbled into the interview on the basis of an inquiry at his college's Office of Career Services. The Office of Career Services was uniformly derided by the graduates of his college as being of no help whatsoever in securing gainful employment.

1. How many times had John been to New York as a child?
    a. Zero.          b. Once.
    c. Several.       d. Too many to count.

2. How did graduates of John's college feel about the Office of Career Services?
    a. Reverent.      b. Unsure.
    c. Ambivalent.    d. Disrespectful.

Still, John had nothing better to do than ask them for assistance, so he dropped in one day. "Hello," said John. "I just finished up my schooling here. I did very well and I am ready to get a job. Can you help me?" The staff looked at him with skepticism, noting his ragged clothes, scraggly beard and unkempt hair. They told John they would do what they could. He doubted them.

1. How did John contact the Office of Career Services for help?
    a. Letter.        b. E-mail..
    c. Telephone      d. Personal visit.

2. Based on the description of John's clothes, which of the following items was he most likely to be wearing?
    a. Necktie.       b. Suit coat.
    c. Torn jeans.    d. Polo shirt.

But, just days later, his phone rang. It was someone from the Office of Career Services. The caller gave John a phone number and an admonition: "This is your chance. Take advantage of it." The number directed him to someone handling staffing for a small investment banking firm in New York City. They needed an analyst, an entry-level position that would require long hours but open up the possibility of becoming a millionaire in under a decade. John just needed work.

1. How did the Office of Career Services contact John?
    a. Letter.        b. E-mail.
    c. Telephone.     d. Personal visit.

2. What else did the Office of Career Services give John when they gave him the phone number of a potential employer?
   a. A warning.
   b. Encouragement.
   c. A small amount of money.
   d. A phone card.

スピードリーディングで読んだものと同じ文を読みます。各設問に対して最も適切な答えを選びなさい。

### 読解問題

John had never been to New York City before his interview to be an investment banker. It was the first job interview he had after graduating from college, his first attempt to translate his education into an occupation. John stumbled into the interview on the basis of an inquiry at his college's Office of Career Services. The Office of Career Services was uniformly derided by the graduates of his college as being of no help whatsoever in securing gainful employment.

Still, John had nothing better to do than ask them for assistance, so he dropped in one day. "Hello," said John. "I just finished up my schooling here. I did very well and I am ready to get a job. Can you help me?" The staff looked at him with skepticism, noting his ragged clothes, scraggly beard and unkempt hair. They told John they would do what they could. He doubted them.

But, just days later, his phone rang. It was someone from the Office of Career Services. The caller gave John a phone number and an admonition: "This is your chance. Take advantage of it." The number directed him to someone handling staffing for a small investment banking firm in New York City. They needed an analyst, an entry-level position that would require long hours but open up the possibility of becoming a millionaire in under a decade. John just needed work.

He called and talked briefly with the bankers and then sent them a resume, transcripts and a writing sample. They called back immediately. "We can't understand why they didn't send you to us sooner," said the folks in New York. John looked in the mirror and imagined what he would look like with all of the hair on his face and most of what was on his head gone. He told the bankers, "I don't know either."

Comprehension Questions

1. How hard was it for John to get his first job interview?
   a. No way to tell.
   b. Easy.
   c. Difficult.
   d. Toughest thing he had ever done.

2. How does the author describe John's general appearance?
   a. Unremarkable.
   b. Tidy.
   c. Sloppy.
   d. Fashionable.

3. Which reaction did John most likely experience when the Office of Career Services contacted him?
   a. Shock.
   b. Pleasant surprise.
   c. Joy.
   d. Confusion.

4. In what industry does John interview for a job?
   a. Entertainment.
   b. Tourism.
   c. Finance.
   d. Manufacturing.

## Part 6　Error Recognition／誤文訂正問題

各文には文法的な誤りがあります。訂正もしくは書き換えを必要とする語や語句を選びなさい。

1. The police <u>responded</u> to the <u>alarm</u> within two minutes and gave <u>pursuing</u> to <u>suspects</u> in a black car.
　　　　　　A　　　　　　　　B　　　　　　　　　　　　　　C　　　　　　D

    解説：give pursuit to ＋名詞で「〜を追跡する」という表現。よって pursuing を pursuit に直す。

    正しい英文：The police responded to the alarm within two minutes and gave pursuit to suspects in a black car.

2. <u>Although</u> she <u>enjoyed</u> the company of her aunt, Kathy wasn't <u>able</u> to visit her as <u>frequency</u> as she would like.
　　A　　　　　　B　　　　　　　　　　　　　　　　　　　　　　C　　　　　　　　D

    解説：as … as 構文は真ん中に形容詞もしくは副詞が来るのが通常。しかし、本文は frequency と名詞が挟まっている。よって frequency を副詞の frequently に直す。

    正しい英文：Although she enjoyed the company of her aunt, Kathy wasn't able to visit her as frequently as she would like.

3. No, he <u>literal</u> fell on his face. He <u>tripped</u> over an extension cord and was <u>not able</u> to <u>catch</u> himself.
　　　　　A　　　　　　　　　　　　B　　　　　　　　　　　　　　　　C　　　　　D

    解説：主語と動詞の間に位置し、動詞を修飾できる語が副詞なので、1つ目の下線部の形容詞 literal を副詞 literally のに直すことで文章が成り立つ。

    正しい英文：No, he literally fell on his face. He tripped over an extension cord and was not able to catch himself.

4. Although it <u>appeared</u> <u>inevitable</u>, I hoped that our class would not have <u>to performing</u> the same program <u>again</u>.
　　　　　　　A　　　　　B　　　　　　　　　　　　　　　　　　　　　C　　　　　　　　　　　　D

    解説：have to で「〜しないといけない」で、to は不定詞なので原形動詞が後に続く。よって performing を perform に直す。

    正しい英文：Although it appeared inevitable, I hoped that our class would not have to perform the same program again.

5. The Clydesdale <u>horses</u> I saw <u>drawing</u> the wagons are not <u>merely</u> big, they are <u>massively</u>.
　　　　　　　　A　　　　　　B　　　　　　　　　　　　C　　　　　　　　　D

    解説：massively は副詞なのに修飾する動詞も形容詞も文中には見当たらない。よって、副詞を形容詞に直す。

    正しい英文：The Clydesdale horses I saw drawing the wagons are not merely big, they are massive.

6. We were <u>astonished</u> to learn that the Lady Grizzly basketball team had <u>not made</u> it into the playoffs. The
　　　　　　　A　　　　　　　　　　　　　　　　　　　　　　　　　　　B

    team <u>had played</u> <u>exceptional</u> well all season.
　　　　　C　　　　　　D

    解説：well を修飾できるのは副詞なのに exceptional が形容詞である。よって副詞形の exceptionally に直す。

    正しい英文：We were astonished to learn that the Lady Grizzly basketball team had not made it into the playoffs. The team had played exceptionally well all season.

7. Let me give you a <u>tipped</u>; don't try to talk to her <u>before</u> 8:00 a.m. She is not a <u>morning</u> person and can be
   　　　　　　　　　　　A　　　　　　　　　　　　　　　　　B　　　　　　　　　　　　　　　C
   a little <u>moody</u>.
   　　　　　D

   解説：give ＋人＋目的語で「人に〜をあげる」。しかし本文では目的語になる部分が過去分詞になっている。よって tipped を名詞の tip に置き換える。

   正しい英文：Let me give you a tip; don't try to talk to her before 8:00 a.m. She is not a morning person and can be a little moody.

# Part 7　Incomplete Sentence／文法・語彙問題

文法的に適切な語や語句を1つ選び、文を完成させなさい。

1. The UN's Kyoto Protocol has been _____ crippled by a walkout by the United States.
    a. virtual	b. to virtual
    c. to virtually	d. virtually

    訳：国連の京都議定書は米国の撤退により事実上その効力を失った。
    解説：has been crippledは現在完了受動態で「不能になった」という意味だが、選択肢の語が「実質上」という意味の語で、動詞のcrippleを修飾しようとしていることから、Dのvirtuallyを選ぶのが最も正しい答えとなる。

2. In the United States, there seems to be an _____ of people with an Irish heritage on Saint Patrick's Day.
    a. explode	b. explosive
    c. explosion	d. exploded

    訳：アメリカ合衆国ではセイントパトリックスデーになるとアイルランドの伝統を祝う群集でごったがえすようだ。
    解説：冠詞に続き、後方から下線部を修飾しているので下線部には単数形名詞が入るのがわかる。よって正解はCになる（注釈：A 動詞、B 形容詞、C 名詞、D 過去分詞）。

3. Mrs. Black taught her fifth grade art class linear perspective by having them use _____ lines.
    a. to intersection	b. intersecting
    c. to intersect	d. intersections

    訳：ブラック先生は5年生の図工のクラスで2本の線を交差させて描く1次遠近法を教えた。
    解説：使役動詞＋人＋原形動詞＋目的語の構文なので下線部とlinesは目的語でないといけないことから下線部がlineを修飾している語であるとわかるので、現在分詞のB「交差している」を選ぶ。

4. If a person has put forth her best effort, I don't believe there is _____ in failure.
    a. shamed	b. shameful
    c. shame	d. shaming

    訳：もし人が全力で挑んだのなら、失敗したとしてもそれは恥ではないと思う。
    解説：There isで「～がある」という意味なので主語となる名詞が来なくてはならない。shamingは不自然な言い回し。よって単純に名詞のCを選ぶ。

5. The teacher noted that the young boy had grown in maturity and now seemed _____ to assume new responsibilities.
    a. preparation	b. in preparation
    c. to prepared	d. prepared

    訳：その少年が大人らしく成長して新しい責任を与えられても大丈夫な様子である、と先生は言った。
    解説：seem＋形容詞で「～のようだ」。選択肢に形容詞がないように見えるが、preparedは「準備のできた」という形容詞。よってDを選ぶ。

# Lesson 4 （http://audio.lincenglish.com にアクセスして音声を聞いてください）

## Part 1　Image Listening／写真描写問題

1. 左の写真を見て、人物の行動や物の位置などについて文を3つ作りなさい。
   _____
   _____
   _____

2. 写真の描写文として最も適切な文をA～Dの中から選びなさい。
   （A），（B），（C），（D）

1. 左の写真を見て、人物の行動や物の位置などについて文を3つ作りなさい。
   _____
   _____
   _____

2. 写真の描写文として最も適切な文をA～Dの中から選びなさい。
   （A），（B），（C），（D）

1. 左の写真を見て、人物の行動や物の位置などについて文を3つ作りなさい。
   _____
   _____
   _____

2. 写真の描写文として最も適切な文をA～Dの中から選びなさい。
   （A），（B），（C），（D）

1. 左の写真を見て、人物の行動や物の位置などについて文を3つ作りなさい。
   _____
   _____
   _____

2. 写真の描写文として最も適切な文をA～Dの中から選びなさい。
   （A），（B），（C），（D）

# Part 2　Question and Response／質疑応答問題

## 重要な質問表現

When did you fall asleep last night?
　　　fall asleep「眠りにつく」。

Will you do a favor for me?
　　　do a favor for a person は do a person a favor「人の頼みを聞いてやる」ということ。

How can I persuade you to change your mind?
　　　persuade you to ～「あなたを説得して～させる」。

Did you mean to imply that I was silly?
　　　imply「ほのめかす・それとなく伝える」。

How can the company promote its product?
　　　promote「販売を促進する」。

When did you eat the entire carton of ice cream?
　　　carton「容器・箱」。

She arranged our flights for the trip.
　　　arrange「手配する・用意する」。

She arranged our flights for the trip.
　　　arrange「手配する・用意する」。

Did the movie frighten you?
　　　frighten「ぎょっとさせる・おびえさせる」。

Have you lived here for more than a decade?
　　　decade「10年間」。

How many items did you purchase?
　　　purchase ＝ buy「買う・購入する」。

## 確認ドリル

次の1～5の質問に対して最も適切な応答をそれぞれ（A）～（C）の中から選びなさい。

1. What shall I do with these useless items?
　（A）　Keep the valuable ones.
　（B）　They are so mysterious.
　（C）　Throw them away.

2. Where do you feel pain?
　（A）　In the refrigerator.
　（B）　By the passage.
　（C）　In my back.

3. Is it true that wisdom comes with age?
　（A）　Nevertheless, he is a passenger on an airplane.
　（B）　Only through experience can someone gain wisdom.
　（C）　I wonder if she has the wisdom to stop.

4. Who is your favorite female singer?
　（A）　He is evil.
　（B）　I can't choose.
　（C）　They are superior.

5. When do you intend to arrive?
　（A）　I graduate next year.
　（B）　I hope to finish the project.
　（C）　I plan to be there by noon.

# Part 3  Short Conversation ／会話問題

次の会話を聞いて、質問に最も適当な答えを選びなさい。

### 質問文パターン

* When 型パターン

1. **A**：Have you had time to respond to the e-mail from your parents, Chris?
   **B**：No, I have so much to accomplish before Friday that I haven't written to them. Right now I'm preparing for a speech that I'll present in class tomorrow.
   **A**：I'll remind you to catch up on your e-mail this weekend.

   **Q**：When will Chris respond to his parents' e-mail?
     a. Before Friday.  b. During the holiday.
     c. During the weekend.  d. Before the speech.

   解説：親からの電子メールに返事を出すのは、週末になりそうである。

* Why 型パターン

2. **A**：You have won so many awards for your work in helping homeless people. You deserve to feel very proud of your efforts, Stan.
   **B**：Actually, Margaret, I'm just glad that I've been able to assist those who don't have a place to live.
   **A**：You remind me to appreciate my own comfortable home.

   **Q**：Why does Stan's work remind Margaret to appreciate her own home?
     a. Because he has helped homeless people.  b. Because he deserves to feel very proud.
     c. Because he is comfortable.  d. Because he has won many awards.

   解説：スタンが、ホームレスの人たちを助けたことで、マーガレットは自分の家の良さに気づいた。

* What 型パターン

3. **A**：I heard about the death of Dan's brother. I'd like to convey my sadness to Dan, but I'm not sure what is considered appropriate.
   **B**：Many people convey their sympathy by sending a card or flowers. You can also take food to the home of the family.
   **A**：Thanks for your suggestions. I'll look for a bouquet of flowers.

   **Q**：What is the purpose of sending a card or flowers in this situation?
     a. To hear about death.  b. To convey sympathy.
     c. To take food.  d. To cause death.

   解説：この場合、カードや花束を贈る目的は、convey their sympathy「お悔やみを伝える」ため。

How 型パターン

4. **A**：Susan was so upset this afternoon. She had lost her coat and then failed a test. It's unusual for her to be disturbed by depressing events. She's usually so optimistic.
   **B**：What can we do to cheer her up?
   **A**：Let's begin by inviting her to go out to dinner. We'll make it a pleasant evening.

   **Q**：How did Susan feel after losing her coat and failing a test?
   　　　a. Optimistic.　　b. Cheerful.
   　　　c. Disturbed.　　d. Pleasant.

解説：スーザンは、コートをなくし、テストも落としたあと、動揺していました。

# Part 4  Short Talks／説明文問題

次の説明文の質問に最も適当な答えを選びなさい。

### アメリカ人コメディアン Bobby Lee

Bobby Lee is a popular American comedian who stars on the television comedy show *MadTV*. He was born in 1972 to parents who emigrated from Korea. When he was a child, his parents expected him to take over their clothing store when he became an adult. However, when he was in college he was discovered by a man who owned a comedy club. The man thought he was very funny and introduced him to other comedians who helped him find more work. In 2001, Bobby started to work on *MadTV* and quickly became one of the most famous comedians on the show. He often plays characters from different Asian countries. In real-life, Bobby loves to golf and he is very generous. In fact, one time he told his audience that he would buy everyone dinner after the show. He is as generous as he is funny.

1. What did his parents expect him to do when he grew up?
    a. Work at a bank.
    b. Move to their homeland in Korea.
    c. Run the family's clothing store.
    d. Be a comedian.

2. Why does Bobby have the reputation of being generous?
    a. Because his comedy shows give away prizes.
    b. Because he bought his whole audience dinner.
    c. Because he often helps homeless people.
    d. Because he pays for his friends' golf lessons.

解説： 設問1　expect 人＋to 動詞で「人が〜することと思う、期待する」という意味。彼の両親は、ボビー・リーが洋服屋を継ぐものだと思っていた。正解－（C）

設問2　ボビー・リーが寛大であるという評判は、彼が観客全員に夕食をご馳走したという事実に基づいたものだ。generous は「寛大な、気前がよい」という意味。正解－（B）

### アメリカン・シンガー Pink

Pink is a popular American singer who has a unique style. Her real name is Alecia Beth Moore, and she grew up in Philadelphia, Pennsylvania. When she was a young girl, her father played guitar and sang to her, which she has said was an inspiration to her. When she was little, she used to run through the house singing loudly. At the age of thirteen, she was hired by a hip-hop musician to be a backup dancer. She then began to sing for his group. After some time, Pink realized she would like to quit the group and pursue a singing career on her own. She loved to write songs, which helped her deal with some difficult times in her past. Pink often has her hair dyed bright pink, which goes with her name. A few years ago, she asked her husband to marry her. He was in a motorcycle race, and when he came around the corner, she held up a sign that said, "Marry Me." They were married the next year. Pink is a very interesting, talented woman.

1. Why did Pink begin to write songs?
  a. Because it helped her deal with her past.
  b. Because her boss asked her to write songs.
  c. Because she wanted to make a lot of money.
  d. Because she wanted to be in a singing group.

2. How did Pink ask her husband to marry her?
  a. She rode up on his motorcycle and asked him.
  b. She took him to a nice dinner and asked him.
  c. She asked him while she was on stage at her concert.
  d. She held up a sign during his motorcycle race.

正解：1－(A)　2－(D)

解説：設問1　質問が聞いているのは、ピンクが歌を書く動機である。本文中にあるように、歌を書くことが helped her deal with some difficult times in her past「過去の困難を乗り越える助けになった」から。正解－(A)

  設問2　ピンクはご主人のバイクのレース中に、Marry Me「結婚してくれ」と書いた札を掲げて結婚を申し込んだのである。Realize「気が付く」。正解－(D)

## Part 5  Reading／読解演習

次の段落文を読み、各設問に対して最も適切な答えを選びなさい（各段落速読問題は2分以内に終わらせなさい）。

### スピードリーディング

Jeremy is a writer who lives in a small town in Montana. In most ways, the town is characteristic of many other small towns in the United States. It is very different from where Jeremy was born, Chicago, which is the third-largest city in the United States. Both of his parents are university professors, which means that Jeremy spent a lot of his childhood in the company of people who were interested in learning. He performed exceptionally in school when he was in high school and went to college at Harvard University.

1. In which field do Jeremy's parents work?
    a. Education.        b. Sales.
    c. Investments.      d. Government.

2. How was Jeremy's academic performance in high school?
    a. Dismal.           b. Below average.
    c. Above average.    d. Superb.

While he attended university, Jeremy studied literature and history, choices that require a great deal of reading and reflect his love of the written word. Jeremy also learned about drawing cartoons and how to write humorously when he worked at the *Lampoon*, a satirical newspaper that Harvard students publish. His cartoons were good enough that Jeremy received a fellowship that allowed him to travel in Europe for a year, studying its art and culture.

1. Which of the following items would be most helpful to Jeremy's study of literature?
    a. Calculator.       b. Jogging shoes.
    c. Dictionary.       d. Scale.

2. What do the writers of the *Lampoon* hope that readers will do?
    a. Become active in politics.    b. Make better investing decisions.
    c. Laugh out loud.               d. Recycle the newspaper.

When he returned to the United States, Jeremy settled in Chicago. He worked for a software company and earned a good living during the first Internet boom. While he was working at that job, Jeremy wrote freelance articles for newspapers in Chicago; he also drew cartoons that would sometimes be published. It was a good life but not the one Jeremy wanted. One day, he decided to leave Chicago and moved to Montana.

1. What did Jeremy do when he came home from Europe?
    a. Lived in his hometown.        b. Traveled in the United States.
    c. Returned to Europe.           d. Finished college.

2. Sometimes, Jeremy's cartoons were _____ by newspapers in Chicago.
   a. illustrated     b. printed
   c. misunderstood   d. presented

スピードリーディングで読んだものと同じ文を読みます。各設問に対して最も適切な答えを選びなさい。

> 読解問題

Jeremy is a writer who lives in a small town in Montana. In most ways, the town is characteristic of many other small towns in the United States. It is very different from where Jeremy was born, Chicago, which is the third-largest city in the United States. Both of his parents are university professors, which means that Jeremy spent a lot of his childhood in the company of people who were interested in learning. He performed exceptionally in school when he was in high school and went to college at Harvard University.

While he attended university, Jeremy studied literature and history, choices that require a great deal of reading and reflect his love of the written word. Jeremy also learned about drawing cartoons and how to write humorously when he worked at the *Lampoon*, a satirical newspaper that Harvard students publish. His cartoons were good enough that Jeremy received a fellowship that allowed him to travel in Europe for a year, studying its art and culture.

When he returned to the United States, Jeremy settled in Chicago. He worked for a software company and earned a good living during the first Internet boom. While he was working at that job, Jeremy wrote freelance articles for newspapers in Chicago; he also drew cartoons that would sometimes be published. It was a good life but not the one Jeremy wanted. One day, he decided to leave Chicago and moved to Montana.

As it turned out, the town where Jeremy moved had a university with a program for writers. Jeremy took one class at the university and liked it, so he applied to attend full-time. He was accepted and spent the next two years writing, learning about writing and teaching others to write. Now it is Jeremy's dream to write a novel, a book about fictional characters that relates something important about the real world. Finishing the book will require perseverance, but Jeremy spends every morning writing for four hours so he can get it done and feels confident in his future success.

Comprehension Questions

1. What kind of environment did Jeremy grow up in?
   a. Rural.     b. Urban.
   c. Rich.      d. Poor.

2. Which of the following did Jeremy do to show his love for writing while he was in college?
   a. Studied creative writing.   b. Composed lengthy letters to friends.
   c. Worked at a newspaper.      d. Wrote a novel.

3. Which emotion describes how Jeremy felt living in Chicago after college?
   a. Elation.      b. Boredom.
   c. Discontent.   d. Malice.

4. Which subject did Jeremy teach when he studied writing in Montana?
   a. History.       b. Mathematics.
   c. Composition.   d. Computer science.

# Part 6 Error Recognition／誤文訂正問題

各文には文法的な誤りがあります。訂正もしくは書き換えを必要とする語や語句を選びなさい。

1. We were asked to <u>initials</u> the document to <u>indicate</u> that we had read, and <u>presumably</u> understood, the <u>risks</u>.
                          A                            B                                  C                              D

    解説：ask は不定詞をとる他動詞なので、to に続く initials は名詞であり、間違いである。よって initials を原形の initial に直す。

    正しい英文：We were asked to initial the document to indicate that we had read, and presumably understood, the risks.

2. The deer posed <u>silently</u> under the elm and <u>fixed</u> me with a <u>steady</u> and vigilant <u>gazed</u>.
                           A                               B                 C                 D

    解説：with ＋ a とくれば最終的に名詞で締めくくられないといけないので、過去分詞の gazed は間違い。よって gazed を名詞の gaze「注視」に直す。

    正しい英文：The deer posed silently under the elm and fixed me with a steady and vigilant gaze.

3. No, I didn't hear the <u>unemployed</u> rate on the <u>economic</u> news. I only <u>caught</u> the <u>interest rate</u>.
                               A                        B                    C             D

    解説：unemployment rate で「失業率」。よって、unemployed を unemployment に直す。

    正しい英文：No, I didn't hear the unemployment rate on the economic news. I only caught the interest rate.

4. We all know what a <u>dares</u> is. Does anyone <u>know</u> what the <u>idiom</u> "double dog <u>dare</u>" means?
                         A                         B              C                 D

    解説：1 つ目の下線部が冠詞 a に続き、それでいて複数形の -s が付いているのでおかしい。よって dares を単数形の dare に直す。

    正しい英文：We all know what a dare is. Does anyone know what the idiom "double dog dare" means?

5. The news <u>reporter</u> alluded to the <u>captured</u> of the head terrorist, but he stopped short of <u>stating</u> that the
                  A                               B                                                                 C

    man was in <u>custody</u>.
                      D

    解説：2 つ目の下線部が the に続き、of で後方からも修飾されているので名詞が来なければいけないのがわかる。よって過去分詞の captured を capture に直す。

    正しい英文：The news reporter alluded to the capture of the head terrorist, but he stopped short of stating that the man was in custody.

6. When I <u>attempted</u> <u>to confirming</u> the news story, I was stonewalled and <u>found</u> my <u>efforts</u> futile.
                 A        B                                                           C           D

    解説：一般動詞 attempt 次に前置詞 to が来ているので、続く confirming が不定詞の形式で原形動詞でないといけないので、confirming を confirm に直す。

正しい英文：When I attempted to confirm the news story, I was stonewalled and found my efforts futile.

7. My cat has begun <u>imitating</u> dogs. Not only does he <u>chew</u> on my shoes, he is showing <u>aggression</u> toward
         　　　　　　　　A　　　　　　　　　　　　　　　　　　B　　　　　　　　　　　　　　　C
   the <u>mailing</u> carrier.
         D

   解説：a mail carrier で「郵便配達員」。よって、the mailing carrier はおかしい。

   正しい英文：My cat has begun imitating dogs. Not only does he chew on my shoes, he is showing aggression toward the mail carrier.

# Part 7  Incomplete Sentence／文法・語彙問題

文法的に適切な語句を1つ選び、文を完成させなさい。

1. I asked that my bill _____ in consideration of payments I recently made.
    a. adjust
    b. be adjusted
    c. to adjust
    d. adjusted

   訳：I asked for my bill だった場合、to be adjusted と言えるが、本文が I asked that my bill となっているので to be adjusted の to は不必要になる。よって be adjusted の B が正解。
   解説：先日支払った分を考慮にいれて、請求書を訂正し直すようにお願いした。

2. Pardon me for _____ . Did you happen to see Clarice come in? I need to speak with her.
    a. interrupt
    b. interruptions
    c. interrupting
    d. interrupted

   訳：ちょっとすみませんが、クレリスを見かけませんでしたか？ 彼女に話したいことがあるんです。
   解説：Pardon me for ＋名詞で「～を許してください」と言う意味。よって前置詞 for の後は名詞が来ないといけないので、BかCが正解となるが、interruption と言う名詞が不加算名詞なので B は間違いになる。

3. My _____ vacation would be a year's trip abroad, traveling wherever and whenever I wanted.
    a. ultimate
    b. is ultimate
    c. be ultimate
    d. being ultimate

   訳：最高の休暇とはおそらく1年かけて、自分が行きたい時に、行きたい所に海外旅行へ行くことでしょう。
   解説：代名詞の所有格 My と名詞の間にあてはまる語が、名詞を修飾する形容詞であることから、主部の下線に当てはまる語が A の ultimate「至極の」しかない。

4. I recall as a child _____ my ABC's into the sand with pine needles. The memory evokes the smell of the salt air.
    a. to trace
    b. traced
    c. tracing
    d. traces

   訳：子供の頃は松の葉で砂に ABC をなぞって書いたものだ。その思い出が潮風の匂いを思い起こさせる。
   解説：recall が文の動詞なので、再び動詞が来る場合、不定詞か分詞形でないといけない。trace は「なぞる」という意味で「なぞったことを思い出す」と言いたいので、不定詞だと副詞用法で「なぞるため」とおかしくなるので、現在分詞の C が正解。

5. Tell me, is it appropriate to include a photograph of oneself with an _____ for employment?
    a. apply
    b. application
    c. applying
    d. applicant

   訳：仕事の応募書類に自分の写真を同封するのは適当か教えてください。
   解説：冠詞 an があるので、単純に単数名詞を探す。よって B が正解。

# Lesson 5 （http://audio.lincenglish.com にアクセスして音声を聞いてください）

## Part 1　Image Listening／写真描写問題

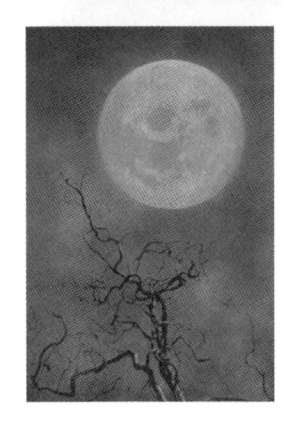

1. 左の写真を見て、人物の行動や物の位置などについて文を3つ作りなさい。
　_____
　_____
　_____

2. 写真の描写文として最も適切な文を A〜D の中から選びなさい。
　（A），（B），（C），（D）

1. 左の写真を見て、人物の行動や物の位置などについて文を3つ作りなさい。
　_____
　_____
　_____

2. 写真の描写文として最も適切な文を A〜D の中から選びなさい。
　（A），（B），（C），（D）

1. 左の写真を見て、人物の行動や物の位置などについて文を3つ作りなさい。
　_____
　_____
　_____

2. 写真の描写文として最も適切な文を A〜D の中から選びなさい。
　（A），（B），（C），（D）

1. 左の写真を見て、人物の行動や物の位置などについて文を3つ作りなさい。
　_____
　_____
　_____

2. 写真の描写文として最も適切な文を A〜D の中から選びなさい。
　（A），（B），（C），（D）

# Part 2　Question and Response／質疑応答問題

## 重要な質問表現

I recommended that she begin now.
　　　　recommend「勧める・奨励する」。

Are those insects annoying you?
　　　　insect「昆虫・虫」。

What kind of diet did the doctor recommend?
　　　　diet「食品・食事・ダイエット制限食」。

No, they do not go together well.
　　　　together「（色などが）調和する」。

Did you make a false statement?
　　　　make a statement「声明を発表する、発言をする」。

From which country does the United States import bananas?
　　　　import「輸入する」。

What is the sum of 20 and 10?
　　　　sum「合計・総計」。

Is "curiosity killed the cat" a proverb?
　　　　"curiosity killed the cat"「好奇心は猫をも殺す・好奇心はほどほどに」。

Why did you take this clock apart?
　　　　take apart「分解する」。

Do you like contemporary art?
　　　　contemporary「現代の」。

## 確認ドリル

次の1～5の質問に対して最も適切な応答をそれぞれ（A）～（C）の中から選びなさい。

1. Did you make an error when you added those numbers?
   (A) Yes, I didn't notice the last number.
   (B) No, I do not want an additional one.
   (C) Yes, I like that advertisement.

2. Can you smell the flowers?
   (A) Yes, I plan to buy flowers tomorrow.
   (B) No, I'm sick with a cold.
   (C) Maybe his laughter was difficult to hear.

3. Was the audience impressed by the politician's speech?
   (A) The audience sat in the front rows of the theater.
   (B) I am listening to a speech.
   (C) Their response was positive.

4. How do I reserve a book at the library?
   (A) Ask the clerk at the library desk.
   (B) Look on the last page of the book.
   (C) Select the library book carefully.

5. Why are you proud?
   (A) Because of fate.
   (B) Because violence is frightening.
   (C) Because I overcame difficulties.

## Part 3　Short Conversation／会話問題

次の会話を聞いて、質問に最も適当な答えを選びなさい。

> 質問文パターン

\* When 型パターン

1. **A**：That politician is emerging as a strong leader in the community.
   **B**：When he states his opinion, people listen.
   **A**：He received a high proportion of the votes in the last election, too.

   **Q**：When will the politician become a strong community leader?
   　　　a. A while ago.　　　b. He is in the process of becoming a strong leader.
   　　　c. No one likes him.　　d. He received a lot of votes in the last election.

　解説：その政治家は、影響力のある指導者として浮上してきているところなので、実際に指導者となるのは、少し先である。

\* How 型パターン

2. **A**：I hope to obtain my driver's license next week. I'll complete the written test and then do the driving section of the test. If I pass both, I'll receive the official license in the mail.
   **B**：How did you learn to drive?
   **A**：In high school I took a course called Driver's Education.

   **Q**：How is the driver's license obtained?
   　　　a. By passing tests.　　　b. By taking a course called Driver's Education.
   　　　c. By driving on a special road.　　d. By filling out a form.

　解説：運転免許証は、筆記および実地の、両方の試験に合格することによって取得できる。

\* Why 型パターン

3. **A**：That party was terrible. The music was too loud, there was too little food, and too many people came for the size of the house.
   **B**：That's why John and I left so early. We went to the Corner House and had coffee instead.
   **A**：I didn't stay late, either. However, I heard that the loud music disturbed the neighbors, and they complained.

   **Q**：Why did people leave the party early?
   　　　a. Because it was very bad.　　　b. Because they wanted coffee instead.
   　　　c. Because the neighbors complained.　　d. Because there was too much food.

　解説：人びとがパーティーから早く帰ったのは、terrible「ひどかった」からである。That's why で「それが〜

の理由で〜する」と言う意味。

* **Where 型パターン**

4. **A**：I bought our tickets for the basketball game on Friday night.
   **B**：Good. I hope you were able to get good seats.
   **A**：We're in the fifth row, almost in back of the coach. They are excellent seats.

   **Q**：Where are the excellent seats for the basketball game?
   　　a. In the fifth row.　　b. In a row.
   　　c. In the new seats.　　d. On the floor.

   解説：バスケットボールの試合で絶好の席とは、in the fifth row, almost in back of the coach「5列目で、ほぼコーチの後ろ」。

# Part 4  Short Talks／説明文問題

次の説明文の質問に最も適当な答えを選びなさい。

### 歯の磨き方の歴史

People have been using different methods of cleaning their teeth for more than 5,000 years. In 3500 B.C., Babylonians used wood sticks called "chewing sticks" to chew on after meals. This practice lasted for thousands of years, changing little over time. People used sticks from trees that were good at freshening breath and used the sharp ends to pick the food out of their teeth. In the 1400s, the Chinese invented the first modern toothbrush made of hair from a wild pig. Europeans brought the idea home and switched from pig hair to horse hair, which was softer. Finally, nylon was invented in 1937, and from then on toothbrushes in the United States and in many parts of the world have been made of this material. Some cultures, however, continue to use the same "chewing sticks" that were used so long ago.

1. Who invented the "chewing stick"?
   a. Europeans.    b. Babylonians.
   c. Americans.    d. The Chinese.

2. Of what material are modern toothbrushes made?
   a. Pig hair.    b. Nylon.
   c. Leather.    d. Wood.

解説：設問1　Chewing Stickとは食事の後歯を掃除するために古代Babyloniansが開発した噛むための小枝である。正解−(B)

設問2　Pig Hairは近代初期の中国人によって開発された歯ブラシで、現代はNylonが使用されている。正解−(B)

### ハワイ島の話

The Hawaiian Islands were discovered by the Polynesians in 1000 A.D. They traveled 1,500 miles north from Polynesia using long canoes. They packed their plants and food with them in their boats and bravely headed off into the unknown. When they arrived, they fought each other over the islands. In 1810, King Kamehameha unified the eight islands to be ruled by him, using weapons he bought from the Americans and British. His favorite island was Maui. King Kamehameha once said, "Maui no ka oi," meaning "Maui is the best." According to the people's religion, they believe that God pulled the Hawaiian Islands out of the ocean with a large fishhook. Hawaii became a state in 1959 and today is one of the most popular tourist destinations in the world.

1. How did the Polynesians get to Hawaii?
   a. By canoes.    b. By large ships.
   c. By train.    d. By swimming.

2. Which island was the favorite of King Kamehameha?
    a. Kauai.    b. Oahu.
    c. Hawaii.    d. Maui.

解説：設問1　紀元1000年に、ポリネシア人たちはlong canoeで勇敢にも2,400kmも旅をしてハワイ諸島を発見した。Polynesian「ポリネシア人」。正解－（A）

設問2　8つの島を統治したカメハメハ大王は、「Maui no ka oi」といって、マウイ島を好んだ。正解－（D）

# Part 5　Reading／読解演習

次の段落文を読み、各設問に対して最も適切な答えを選びなさい（各段落速読問題は2分以内に終わらせなさい）。

### スピードリーディング

　Seth is a journalist who lives in Wyoming. He works for a small newspaper in a town where skiing is very popular. In addition to writing, he does a lot of photography. Because the town is located in the mountains, it is very beautiful and there are many publications, not just his own newspaper, that want to print his photographs.

　　1. What type of business does the article mention as being important to Seth's town?
　　　　a. Manufacturing.　　b. Recreation.
　　　　c. Health care.　　　d. Transportation.

　　2. Which word best describes the town where Seth lives?
　　　　a. Gritty.　　b. Tropical.
　　　　c. Urbane.　　d. Scenic.

　Because of this, Seth is thinking about quitting the newspaper and working as a freelance photographer. The benefit of this is that Seth will get to choose what he works on, which means he can choose to take pictures of what is really interesting to him as long as people want to buy those pictures. Not working on the staff of a newspaper, however, means that Seth has no guarantee that he will earn enough money every month to pay his rent and other expenses.

　　1. What would Seth have to do before working as a freelancer?
　　　　a. Exercise his options.　　　b. Spend less time skiing.
　　　　c. Move to a different town.　d. Resign from the newspaper.

　　2. What will be the main benefit of Seth working for himself?
　　　　a. More security.　　b. More recognition.
　　　　c. More freedom.　　d. More excitement.

　One thing that worries Seth a little bit is that he likes to ski so much that he is afraid he will not force himself to photograph a wide enough range of people and places to keep selling all his pictures. When he works at the newspaper, Seth receives assignments from his editor and must complete them whether he wants to or not. Sometimes, his assignments are very interesting even though he never would have imagined that before shooting them. If Seth is picking his own work, he might miss out on this kind of assignment.

　　1. What character trait does Seth believe he will have to develop in order to be successful as a freelancer?
　　　　a. Wisdom.　　b. Self-discipline.
　　　　c. Courage.　　d. Congeniality.

2. How concerned is Seth about not developing the habits to be a good freelancer?
    a. Not at all worried.    b. Not too worried.
    c. Fairly worried.    d. Terribly worried.

スピードリーディングで読んだものと同じ文を読みます。各設問に対して最も適切な答えを選びなさい。

> 読解問題

Seth is a journalist who lives in Wyoming. He works for a small newspaper in a town where skiing is very popular. In addition to writing, he does a lot of photography. Because the town is located in the mountains, it is very beautiful and there are many publications, not just his own newspaper, that want to print his photographs.

Because of this, Seth is thinking about quitting the newspaper and working as a freelance photographer. The benefit of this is that Seth will get to choose what he works on, which means he can choose to take pictures of what is really interesting to him as long as people want to buy those pictures. Not working on the staff of a newspaper, however, means that Seth has no guarantee that he will earn enough money every month to pay his rent and other expenses.

One thing that worries Seth a little bit is that he likes to ski so much that he is afraid he will not force himself to photograph a wide enough range of people and places to keep selling all his pictures. When he works at the newspaper, Seth receives assignments from his editor and must complete them whether he wants to or not. Sometimes, his assignments are very interesting even though he never would have imagined that before shooting them. If Seth is picking his own work, he might miss out on this kind of assignment.

Not having health insurance when he works as a freelancer is also a potential problem for Seth. Because he takes pictures outdoors and often in places that it can be dangerous to get to, there is a chance he could hurt himself. If that happens, he will have to pay very high medical bills at the same time that he will not be able to work in order to pay them. This is a widespread drawback for American workers who wish to become self-employed, because health care is very expensive and is not guaranteed by the government.

Comprehension Questions

1. What type of art does Seth produce?
    a. Three-dimensional.    b. Lexical.
    c. Performing.    d. Visual.

2. At the time of the story, Seth is debating what to do with his _____.
    a. past    b. present
    c. future    d. fortune

3. What will Seth lack without his job at a newspaper?
    a. Any subjects.    b. Necessary equipment.
    c. A boss.    d. Time.

4. Which of the following would eliminate the drawback Seth faces about medical care?
    a. Stronger families.    b. Greater environmental regulations.
    c. Lower taxes.    d. Government insurance.

Lesson 5　55

## Part 6　Error Recognition／誤文訂正問題

各文には文法的な誤りがあります。訂正もしくは書き換えを必要とする語や語句を選びなさい。

1. <u>Whether</u> not huge, our Japanese garden <u>requires</u> constant <u>maintenance</u> to keep it <u>looking</u> nice.
　　　A　　　　　　　　　　　　　　　　　B　　　　　　　　　C　　　　　　　　　　D

　　解説：譲歩の短縮形に While not という構文があることから、whether not がその間違いであると気付く。
　　　　　While it is not huge が短縮される前の形である。

　　正しい英文：While not huge, our Japanese garden requires constant maintenance to keep it looking nice.

2. We <u>think</u> you should <u>to go</u> visit your family in Holland, <u>even if</u> you <u>don't</u> speak Dutch.
　　　　A　　　　　　　　B　　　　　　　　　　　　　　　　　C　　　　　　D

　　解説：should は助動詞なので続く動詞は必ず原形である。よって不定詞の to go を原形動詞の go に正す。

　　正しい英文：We think you should go visit your family in Holland, even if you don't speak Dutch.

3. The <u>candidate</u> gave his acceptance speech <u>shortly</u> after his nomination <u>for</u> that he could begin <u>his</u> campaign work.
　　　　A　　　　　　　　　　　　　　　　B　　　　　　　　　　　　　　C　　　　　　　　　　　　D

　　解説：文中にある for that はおかしい表現。内容から考え、「そうしたら」と言いたいので for that を so
　　　　　that に直す。

　　正しい英文：The candidate gave his acceptance speech shortly after his nomination  so that he could begin
　　　　　　　　his campaign work.

4. Regular <u>service</u> should be <u>done</u> on cars in <u>ordering</u> that their optimum performance be <u>achieved</u>.
　　　　　A　　　　　　　　　B　　　　　　　　　C　　　　　　　　　　　　　　　　　　　　　D

　　解説：in order to ＋原形動詞、もしくは in order that ＋文で「～するために」という熟語。よって in
　　　　　ordering that は誤用法。ordering は order に直されるべきである。

　　正しい英文：Regular service should be done on cars in order that their optimum performance be achieved.

5. You <u>gave</u> up your job so <u>for</u> you could pursue your <u>studies</u> abroad? I wish you the very best of luck <u>in</u> your
　　　　A　　　　　　　　　B　　　　　　　　　　　　C　　　　　　　　　　　　　　　　　　　　　　　　　D
　　endeavors.

　　解説：文中にある so for は不適切な表現。内容から考え、「～できるように」と言いたいので so for を so that
　　　　　に直す。

　　正しい英文：You gave up your job so that you could pursue your studies abroad? I wish you the very best of
　　　　　　　　luck in your endeavors.

6. <u>There</u> have been a lot of bikes <u>stolen</u> from campus lately. If you <u>leaving</u> your bike there, make <u>sure</u> it's locked.
　　　A　　　　　　　　　　　　　B　　　　　　　　　　　　　　　　　　C　　　　　　　　　　　　D

　　解説：2 文目の従属節が現在命令形であるので、主節もそのまま現在形でよいとわかる。よって、leaving を
　　　　　主語の you に合わせ、leave に置き換える。

　　正しい英文：There have been a lot of bikes stolen from campus lately. If you leave your bike there, make sure it's locked.

7. If you <u>should</u> happen <u>to go</u> in the bookstore while <u>your</u> at the mall, will you pick up an <u>inexpensive</u> dictio-
　　　　　 A　　　　　　　 B　　　　　　　　　　　　　　 C　　　　　　　　　　　　　　　　　　　　 D
nary for me?

　　解説：while は「〜する一方」という接続詞。while your at the mall は文法的に考えておかしいので、your が同じ発音の you're の間違いである予想がつく。

　　正しい英文：If you should happen to go in the bookstore while you're at the mall, will you pick up an inexpensive dictionary for me?

# Part 7  Incomplete Sentence ／文法・語彙問題

文法的に適切な語や語句を 1 つ選び、文を完成させなさい。

1. Were it summer vacation, we would have no _____ to complete our homework tonight.
   a. obligatory　　b. oblige
   c. obliging　　d. obligation

   訳：もし今が夏休み中なら、宿題を今夜終わらせなくてはならないという義務を負わされなくてすむのに。
   解説：本文は If ＋過去形、would（could）……「もし～なら、……でしょう。」と言う仮定法過去の文の If を使わない倒置表現である。would の後に have が来ているので仮定法過去完了のようにも思えるが、それに続き、no が来ているので、下線部が have の目的語でないといけないのがわかる。よって選択肢の中から名詞を選ぶ必要がある。C の動名詞は不自然。

2. We couldn't decide _____ it was reasonable to request a second portion of dessert.
   a. whatever　　b. weather
   c. whether　　d. whither

   訳：私達は 2 つ目のデザートを注文するのが果たして賢い選択であるかどうか決めかねていた。
   解説：内容から考えて、「～かどうか」が最も適当なので、C の whether を選ぶ。
   （注釈：A「何でも」B「天気」D「衰える」）

3. We can borrow our father's car unless he's using it, in _____ case we'll have to walk.
   a. what　　b. which
   c. when　　d. where

   訳：父が使っていなければ、車を借りることができます。でも使っていた場合、私たちは歩いて行かなければならないでしょう。
   解説：in which case は接続詞的用法で「その場合には」という慣用句。

4. Your gymnastics routine may consist of any combination of the required movements _____ it does not exceed five minutes in length.
   a. while　　b. ntil
   c. for one thing　　d. as long as

   訳：それぞれの運動を 5 分以上続けてやらない限り、どのように組み合わせてトレーニング表をつくってもかまいません。
   解説：内容から考えて D の「～する限り」が最も適当。（注釈：A「～する間」B「～まで」）D は文法的に合わない。

5. We are privileged to live in this mansion. The view is beautiful and looks out _____ the sea.
   a. under  b. over
   c. until   d. for

訳：私たちがこの豪邸に住めるなんて、特権である。眺めは最高で、海を見渡せるようになっている。

解説：2文目は景色の話をしているので、CとDは合わない。海の底は見えないので、Aのunderは間違い。よってBが最も適切な語である。

## Lesson 6 (http://audio.lincenglish.com にアクセスして音声を聞いてください)

### Part 1　Image Listening／写真描写問題

1. 左の写真を見て、人物の行動や物の位置などについて文を3つ作りなさい。
   _____
   _____
   _____

2. 写真の描写文として最も適切な文をA〜Dの中から選びなさい。
   (A),　(B),　(C),　(D)

1. 左の写真を見て、人物の行動や物の位置などについて文を3つ作りなさい。
   _____
   _____
   _____

2. 写真の描写文として最も適切な文をA〜Dの中から選びなさい。
   (A),　(B),　(C),　(D)

1. 左の写真を見て、人物の行動や物の位置などについて文を3つ作りなさい。
   _____
   _____
   _____

2. 写真の描写文として最も適切な文をA〜Dの中から選びなさい。
   (A),　(B),　(C),　(D)

1. 左の写真を見て、人物の行動や物の位置などについて文を3つ作りなさい。
   _____
   _____
   _____

2. 写真の描写文として最も適切な文をA〜Dの中から選びなさい。
   (A),　(B),　(C),　(D)

# Part 2　Question and Response／質疑応答問題

## 重要な質問表現

Did you finish the entire assignment?
　　entire「すべての・全体の」。

Will you please hang up your coat?
　　Will you ～?「(軽い命令・指示) ～してください・～しませんか」

Why are you bored?
　　bored「退屈して・うんざりして」。

Is there a grocery storey nearby?
　　nearby「すぐそばに・近所に」。

Were you treated fairly?
　　treat「扱う・遇する」。

Is the description of the man's personality correct?
　　description「描写・説明」。

The snow has been falling constantly.
　　constantly「絶えず・しきりに」。

She is very efficient.
　　efficient「有能な・敏腕な」。

How do you feel about his criticism?
　　criticism「批評・批判」。

Did you find a solution to your problem?
　　solution「解決方法」。

## 確認ドリル

次の1～5の質問に対して最も適切な応答をそれぞれ (A)～(C) の中から選びなさい。

1. How can I persuade you to change your mind?
　　(A) You can't. I'm positive that I'm right.
　　(B) I'm glad that you met the politician.
　　(C) His personality is unique.

2. Were you disturbed by the noise?
　　(A) It was a mysterious event.
　　(B) The organization was unknown.
　　(C) I was, so I complained.

3. Do you think she is attractive?
　　(A) Yes, she is critical.
　　(B) Yes, she is beautiful.
　　(C) Yes, she is evil.

4. Have you read that novel?
　　(A) Yes, I enjoyed every page.
　　(B) Yes, I would like to be an author.
　　(C) Yes, I am bored.

5. Have you recovered from your illness?
　　(A) Thank you. I feel much better now.
　　(B) A virus causes the common cold.
　　(C) Yes, the treatment will begin tomorrow.

# Part 3　Short Conversation／会話問題

次の会話を聞いて、質問に最も適当な答えを選びなさい。

## 質問文パターン

### ＊Why 型パターン

1. **A**：Let's go pick some apples from the tree in the yard. I'd like to make a pie for dessert.
   **B**：I was out in the yard yesterday. I think the apples attract insects. Bees, for example, are attracted to sugar, and there's sugar in apples.
   **A**：If we pick the apples, maybe the number of insects will decrease.

   **Q**：Why might insects decrease if the apples are picked?
   　　a. Because the apples are on the tree in the yard.　　b. Because the sugar in the fruit attracts insects.
   　　c. Because a pie is made for dessert.　　d. Because insects can be a problem.

解説：リンゴを取ると虫が減るのは、果物に虫を引き寄せる糖分が含まれているから。

### ＊What 型パターン

2. **A**：I asked several of my friends if they would like to help paint my house, but they gave me a negative response.
   **B**：Painting a house is a lot of work.
   **A**：Nevertheless, I thought someone might be willing. I was wrong.

   **Q**：What did all of his friends say when he asked if they would help paint the house?
   　　a. No.　　b. Yes.
   　　c. Maybe.　　d. Next time.

解説：家の塗装を頼んだとき、they gave me a negative response「良い返事をもらうことができませんでした」。

### ＊How 型パターン

3. **A**：I will arise at sunrise to get an early start for our trip to the beach.
   **B**：Margaret, you're usually asleep at sunrise, so you had better set the alarm clock.
   **A**：I'll set it to ring at 5:00 A.M. That should be early enough.

   **Q**：How will Margaret get an early start on the trip to the beach?
   　　a. Ignore the alarm clock.　　b. Get up at sunrise.
   　　c. Drive the car.　　d. Skip breakfast.

解説：海辺での1日を早く始めるために、マーガレットは日の出に起きるつもりである。

* Which 型パターン
4. **A**：I want to learn how to cross-country ski.
   **B**：You need to know how to hold the poles and how to position your body. Moving your feet properly is the most difficult part.
   **A**：Could you show me what the proper movements are?

   **Q**：Which feature of cross-country skiing is most difficult?
     a. Positioning the body.  b. Correct movement of feet.
     c. Holding the poles.   d. Getting up after falling.

   解説：クロスカントリーの特性で、Moving your feet properly is the most difficult part「適切な足の動かし方が一番難しい点です」。

## Part 4　Short Talks／説明文問題

次の説明文の質問に最も適当な答えを選びなさい。

### オーブン

An oven is an enclosed compartment for heating, baking or drying. It is often used in cooking and pottery. Two common kinds of modern ovens are gas ovens and electric ovens. Almost every house in the United States has an oven in the kitchen. People use ovens daily to cook dinner, such as meat, potatoes, and casseroles. Baking is done in ovens as well. Baking is when you make things usually containing flour, such as cookies, cakes and bread. Ovens used in pottery are also known as kilns. Artists use kilns to create sculptures and other art. Other people use kilns to make bowls, cups, vases and other household items.

1. What is an electric or gas oven often used for?
   a. Heating the house.    b. Starting fires in the fireplace.
   c. Training artists.     d. Cooking casseroles.

2. What kind of oven is used for pottery?
   a. A gas oven.    b. An electric fry pan.
   c. A campfire.    d. A kiln.

解説：設問1　電気やガスのオーブンは、各家庭に1台あるほどアメリカでは一般的で、料理に使用される。正解－(D)
　　　設問2　陶器などを焼くためのオーブンは特にkiln「釜（炉）」と呼ばれ、芸術家たちなどにも使用されている。正解－(D)

### アニマル・シェルター

An animal shelter is a facility that houses homeless, lost or abandoned animals, primarily a large variety of dogs and cats. The animal is kept at the shelter until it is either reclaimed by an owner, adopted to a new owner, placed with another organization, or killed. If an owner loses a pet, the first place he or she should look is at the animal shelter. New pets are held for about a week, in order to give owners a chance to reclaim them. Others will keep an animal for a specific period of time and then put them to sleep in a humane way. Usually this is done by an injection, and it is not painful for the animal. Today, many shelters are adopting a "no-kill" policy, which means they will keep the animals until they are adopted and never put them down.

1. What is an animal shelter?
   a. An umbrella that is made for animals.        b. A building for lost children.
   c. A place that breeds and houses many          d. A facility that houses homeless animals.
      litters of baby animals.

2. How long are the animals kept at an animal shelter?
   a. Until they are picked up by the police.       b. Until they learn how to do tricks.
   c. Until they go to their old home, an adopted   d. After they get enough sleep.
      home, another facility, or are killed.

解説：設問1　Shelterは「住居」という意味で、Animal Shelterは「動物を保護する施設」を指す。正解－(D)
　　　設問2　保護施設では、一定期間動物が保護され、飼い主が見つからなかったり引き取られなかった場合、安楽死をさせてしまうことがある。put ～ to sleep in humane way「安楽死させる」。正解－(C)

# Part 5　Reading ／読解演習

次の段落文を読み、各設問に対して最も適切な答えを選びなさい（各段落速読問題は2分以内に終わらせなさい）。

### スピードリーディング

　Maria Merian was born in northern Europe in 1647 and went on to become a very famous artist and naturalist. Merian studied how caterpillars change into moths and butterflies, a process called metamorphosis, and she did it in ways unlike any studies done by people before her. Merian carefully drew moths and butterflies just as they appeared in nature, placing them on the plants they ate alongside the caterpillar forms they began as. Because photography had not yet been invented, sketches and paintings done by hand were the only way to preserve what an animal looked like.

　　1. Merian was both an artist and _____.
　　　　a. a hunter　　　b. a cook
　　　　c. a scientist　　d. a jeweler

　　2. What about the animals she studied did Merian pay particular attention to?
　　　　a. Clerk.　　　　　　　　b. Where they lived.
　　　　c. How large they got.　　d. When they disappeared.

　Before Merian, and even for a long time afterwards, no one thought it was important to draw animals in their environment the way she did. Merian's dedication to representational integrity set her apart from the other people who studied nature at the same time she did. In those days, most biology was conducted by people who did it as a hobby. Today science is a profession, and it is difficult to make a contribution without many years of education. When Merian was working, almost three centuries ago, so much was not known about the world that anyone with the time and intelligence could learn something no one else knew.

　　1. How was the study of nature regarded at the time Merian did it?
　　　　a. As something dangerous.　　　　　　　　b. As something that paid well.
　　　　c. As something only the poor would want to do.　　d. As something to be done for fun.

　　2. How much education was required to do what Merian did?
　　　　a. No formal education.　　　　　　b. Some basic education.
　　　　c. The equivalent of a college degree.　　d. Very advanced education.

　Merian fit her studies into a busy life; she was a mother of two daughters and in charge of a household in a time long before any modern labor-saving devices had been invented. One of the most amazing things Merian did was that she traveled to South America in 1699 to study insects in the tropical jungles of Surinam, a Dutch colony. The trip was brave for anyone to attempt, but it was especially hard for a woman over fifty years old who was supporting herself.

1. Where did Merian travel in 1699?
    a. Dutch.      b. South America.
    c. Europe.     d. America.

2. What virtue was required of Merian to make her journey?
    a. Kindness.    b. Wisdom.
    c. Generosity.  d. Courage.

スピードリーディングで読んだものと同じ文を読みます。各設問に対して最も適切な答えを選びなさい。

### 読解問題

Maria Merian was born in northern Europe in 1647 and went on to become a very famous artist and naturalist. Merian studied how caterpillars change into moths and butterflies, a process called metamorphosis, and she did it in ways unlike any studies done by people before her. Merian carefully drew moths and butterflies just as they appeared in nature, placing them on the plants they ate alongside the caterpillar forms they began as. Because photography had not yet been invented, sketches and paintings done by hand were the only way to preserve what an animal looked like.

Before Merian, and even for a long time afterwards, no one thought it was important to draw animals in their environment the way she did. Merian's dedication to representational integrity set her apart from the other people who studied nature at the same time she did. In those days, most biology was conducted by people who did it as a hobby. Today science is a profession, and it is difficult to make a contribution without many years of education. When Merian was working, almost three centuries ago, so much was not known about the world that anyone with the time and intelligence could learn something no one else knew.

Merian fit her studies into a busy life; she was a mother of two daughters and in charge of a household in a time long before any modern labor-saving devices had been invented. One of the most amazing things Merian did was that she traveled to South America in 1699 to study insects in the tropical jungles of Surinam, a Dutch colony. The trip was brave for anyone to attempt, but it was especially hard for a woman over fifty years old who was supporting herself.

While Merian was special for her independence in a time long before women were so independent, her perspective on art was the most important and enduring thing about her life. Merian studied not only how the animals that she painted looked but also how they lived. Because Merian's style was unique, her illustrations are more accurate than illustrations by anyone else in her time. Her pictures were as beautiful as they were true.

Comprehension Questions

1. Which word best describes this article about Merian?
    a. Editorial.    b. History.
    c. Promotion.    d. Commercial.

2. Unlike Merian, how do most people who study biology make a living?

  a. Maintaining a household.  b. Drawing and painting.

  c. By studying biology.  d. Teaching mathematics.

3. Which word most closely resembles how the author describes Merian's travel in 1699?

  a. Primitive.  b. Uninteresting.

  c. Remarkable.  d. Plain.

4. How is Merian's artistic style described?

  a. Unlike anyone else's.  b. Good but not great.

  c. Fanciful.  d. Common.

# Part 6　Error Recognition／誤文訂正問題

各文には文法的な誤りがあります。訂正もしくは書き換えを必要とする語や語句を選びなさい。

1. My <u>obligatory</u> to the <u>military</u> will be <u>satisfied</u> in one year, three <u>months</u> and two days.
　　　　A　　　　　　　　B　　　　　　　C　　　　　　　　　　　　　D

    解説：代名詞の所有格 My に続き、それが修飾するはずの名詞がないまま前置詞 to が来ているので、1つ目の下線 obligatory が間違いであることがわかる。よって obligatory を名詞の obligation「義務」に直す。

    正しい英文：My obligation to the military will be satisfied in one year, three months and two days.

2. Why are you <u>throwing</u> out those <u>shelves</u>? It seems a <u>shamed</u> to <u>waste</u> them.
　　　　　　　　　A　　　　　　　　B　　　　　　　　C　　　　D

    解説：2文目の冠詞 a の後に shamed という過去分詞が来ているが、肝心の名詞が見当たらない。よって3つ目の下線部 shamed が名詞の shame であるべきである。

    正しい英文：Why are you throwing out those shelves? It seems a shame to waste them.

3. Do you <u>suppose</u> there is enough <u>interest</u> in ice skating to <u>generates</u> support for public <u>funding</u> of a new rink?
　　　　　　A　　　　　　　　　　　　B　　　　　　　　　　　C　　　　　　　　　　　　　　D

    解説：本文には「〜するために」という不定詞の副詞用法が使われているが、不定詞の形「to ＋原形動詞」がきちんと取れていない。よって generates は generates に訂正されなくてはならない。

    正しい英文：Do you suppose there is enough interest in ice skating to generate support for public funding of a new rink?

4. <u>Ownership</u> of the garage was in <u>disputed</u>. It was <u>evident</u> to me that the two neighbors would be <u>resolving</u>
　　A　　　　　　　　　　　　　　　　B　　　　　　　C　　　　　　　　　　　　　　　　　　　　　　　　　D

    their disagreement in court.

    解説：1文目の in disputed という表現が不自然。in dispute で「未解決の」という言い回しなので、disputed を dispute に直すことで意味が通る。

    正しい英文：Ownership of the garage was in dispute.  It was evident to me that the two neighbors would be resolving their disagreement in court.

5. George, the elderly <u>neighbors</u>, was regularly involved in <u>legal</u> suits. I knew this situation was a <u>ploy</u> to
　　　　　　　　　　A　　　　　　　　　　　　　　　　　B　　　　　　　　　　　　　　　　　　　　　C

    acquire ownership of the <u>building</u>.
　　　　　　　　　　　　　　　D

    解説：George と neighbors は同一のものの言い換えなのに、1つ目の下線部が neighbors と複数形になっている。よって単数の neighbor に直さなければならない。

    正しい英文：George, the elderly neighbor, was regularly involved in legal suits. I knew this situation was a ploy to acqu-ire ownership of the building.

6. The lake was <u>exceptionally</u> beautiful with a mauve fog <u>hanging</u> over it; unfortunately, I did not have film
                    A                                                       B

   that would <u>capturing</u> the subtleties of the <u>colors</u>.
                  C                          D

   解説：助動詞に続く動詞は必ず動詞の原形でなければならないことを理解していれば、間違いは一目瞭然である。3つ目の下線をcaptureに直せば正しい文章になる。

   正しい英文：The lake was exceptionally beautiful with a mauve fog hanging over it; unfortunately, I did not have film that would capture the subtleties of the colors.

7. A <u>massive</u> <u>traffic jam</u> and a great deal of <u>confusion</u> resulted when pranksters removed directional signs at
       A       B                       C

   the site of the road <u>constructed</u>.
                           D

   解説：road constructionで道路工事。また通常、修飾部の前置詞ofは通常名詞で締めくくられるので、過去分詞は不自然なことからも間違いに気が付く。

   正しい英文：A massive traffic jam and a great deal of confusion resulted when pranksters removed directional signs at the site of the road construction.

# Part 7　Incomplete Sentence／文法・語彙問題

文法的に適切な語や語句を1つ選び、文を完成させなさい。

1. For most people, counting by _____ numbers is not as familiar or effortless as counting by even numbers. Try it!
   - a. odd
   - b. odder
   - c. most odd
   - d. oddest

訳：奇数で数える方法は多くの人には馴染みがなく、偶数で数えるほど容易ではありません。試しにやってみてください。

解説：下線部が後半のcounting by even numbers「偶数で数える」と対比しているので、同じ形でないといけない even numberが偶数でodd numberが奇数なので、Aのoddが正解となる。

2. Clarence has given me _____ no reason to distrust him. My faith in him is unquestionable.
   - a. absolute
   - b. absolutes
   - c. absolution
   - d. absolutely

訳：クラレンスによれば、彼を疑う理由が私には全くなかった。私の彼への信頼は確かなものです。

解説：選択肢の語彙が「完全」と言う意味の語であり、文章のどの言葉を説明しているか考えると、内容からgiveであるのがわかるので、動詞を修飾できる副詞を選択肢から選ぶのが正しい答えになる。よってdが最も正しい答え。

3. Do you remember the game of "telephone" in which a group of children would _____ a statement from one child to the next?
   - a. to whisper
   - b. whispering
   - c. whispers
   - d. whisper

訳：子供達がグループに別れ、次から次へと伝言を囁いて伝えていく「テレフォン」というゲームを覚えていますか？

解説：助動詞に続くので、決まりに従い、下線部には原形動詞が入らなければならない。よってDが正解。

4. We had _____ resolved all of the problems by rescheduling the class for 9:00 a.m.
   - a. effecting
   - b. effectively
   - c. effects
   - d. to effect

訳：クラスを午前の9時に変更する事により、効率的に全ての問題を解決できた。

解説：下線部の前後がhad resolvedと過去完了の正しい形が取れていることから、下線部が動詞を修飾する語の副詞であると考えられる。よって、Bのeffectivelyを選ぶのが正しい答え。

5. It is a sad fact, but I no longer trust the large North American broadcast organizations to be _____ sources of national or international news and information.

    a. reliable  b. reliability
    c. rely   d. relies

訳：悲しいことだが、北アメリカの放送網が報道する国外・国内のニュースが信頼できる情報源であるとはもう思えない。

解説：下線部前にbe動詞があり、下線部後に「情報」という名詞が来ているので、そこから考えると、下線部には名詞を修飾する形容詞が入ることがわかる。よってAがもっとも正しい答え。

# Lesson 7 (http://audio.lincenglish.com にアクセスして音声を聞いてください)

## Part 1　Image Listening／写真描写問題

1. 左の写真を見て、人物の行動や物の位置などについて文を 3 つ作りなさい。
   _____
   _____
   _____

2. 写真の描写文として最も適切な文を A～D の中から選びなさい。
   (A), (B), (C), (D)

1. 左の写真を見て、人物の行動や物の位置などについて文を 3 つ作りなさい。
   _____
   _____
   _____

2. 写真の描写文として最も適切な文を A～D の中から選びなさい。
   (A), (B), (C), (D)

1. 左の写真を見て、人物の行動や物の位置などについて文を 3 つ作りなさい。
   _____
   _____
   _____

2. 写真の描写文として最も適切な文を A～D の中から選びなさい。
   (A), (B), (C), (D)

1. 左の写真を見て、人物の行動や物の位置などについて文を 3 つ作りなさい。
   _____
   _____
   _____

2. 写真の描写文として最も適切な文を A～D の中から選びなさい。
   (A), (B), (C), (D)

# Part 2　Question and Response／質疑応答問題

### 重要な質問表現

Why did the Wweb site deny them access?
　　deny「否認する・否定する」。

What is the lesson that you learned?
　　「教え・教訓」。learn one's lesson で、「教訓を学ぶ」。

How would you describe someone who is a billionaire?
　　billionaire「億万長者」。類義語に millionaire（百万長者・大富豪）がある。

My car had a flat tire.
　　tire「タイヤのパンク」。

Do you have anything to declare?
　　declare「税関などで課税品などを申告する」。アメリカ合衆国へ入国する際、custom declaration form（税関申告書）に記入し、税関検査官へ手渡す必要がある。

Is the puzzle too complicated for you to complete?
　　complicated「複雑な・ややこしい」。

Who is to blame for the accident?
　　to blame「責めを負うべきである」。

The crowd yelled with delight.
　　with delight「喜んで」。

Do you have a permit to park here?
　　permit「許可（証）」。駐車した車の窓辺に提示しておくようである。

I bought it at the drug store.
　　drug store「ドラッグストア」。薬・化粧品・タバコ・文房具などを売る店。

### 確認ドリル

次の 1 〜 5 の質問に対して最も適切な応答をそれぞれ（A）〜（C）の中から選びなさい。

1. What is the subject of the new display at the museum?
　（A）　It will open on Friday.
　（B）　The last time I went I really enjoyed the show.
　（C）　The history of the local Indian tribe.

2. How did you collect so many sea shells?
　（A）　My friend has an even bigger collection of buttons.
　（B）　I like to spend hours looking at thei shapes and patterns.
　（C）　During my vacation, I roamed the beach each morning.

3. What kind of destruction does a tornado cause?
　（A）　Strong winds often destroy crops and homes.
　（B）　The last storm was in April.
　（C）　I have seen one that was huge.

4. Are you willing to do me a favor?
　（A）　I would like to have an orange soda.
　（B）　Sure, anything. Just ask and I'll help out.
　（C）　I like playing games with you.

5. What is the most important skill for scoring in this game?
   (A) Be sure you take careful aim.
   (B) Let your teammate shoot.
   (C) Have fun playing.

# Part 3　Short Conversation／会話問題

次の会話を聞いて、質問に最も適当な答えを選びなさい。

### 質問文パターン

＊What 型パターン

1. **A**：In spite of what you say, I plan to buy you a gift.
   **B**：It's really not necessary.
   **A**：I'm making a choice among jewelry, clothing, or books, although you already have a lot of clothes and books.

   **Q**：What is likely to be purchased?
   　　a. Clothing.　　b. Book.
   　　c. Jewelry.　　d. Nothing.

   解説：in spite of で「～にも関らず、～を無視して、物ともせず」という意味の成句。necessary は「（～には、～のために、～にとって）必要な、なくてはならない、必然の、避けがたい」という意味。
   　　話し手 A は making a choice among jewelry, clothing, or books「宝石、衣服、本の中から決めるつもり」だが、話し手 B は already have a lot of clothes and books「すでに多くの本と衣服を持っている」から。

＊How 型パターン

2. **A**：My physics class conflicts with the party this afternoon. I need to attend the class, but I don't want to miss the party.
   **B**：How about going to class and coming to the party when class is finished?
   **A**：That's an intelligent solution.

   **Q**：How has the conflict been solved?
   　　a. The student will do neither.　　b. The student will attend the party.
   　　c. The student will miss class.　　d. The student will do both.

   解説：conflicts with で「（計画などが）かち合う」という意味。intelligent は「知的な、聡明な、気の利いた」という意味。solution は「解答、解決策」という意味。
   　　学生は going to class and coming to the party when class is finished「授業にでて、授業が終わったらパーティーに来る」ことでかち合いを解決するから。

＊Why 型パターン

3. **A**：She said Tom's grammar was terrible.
   **B**：How can that be? He's a native speaker of English.
   **A**：Not all native speakers have been educated in correct grammar.

**Q**：Why is Tom's grammar poor?
  a. Because he's just learning English.　　b. Because of his education.
  c. Because he speaks English.　　d. Because he usually speaks German.

解説：grammar は「文法、（文法にかなった）語法、（個人の）言葉遣い」という意味。terrible は「ひどい、ひどく悪い、とても下手な」という意味。native speaker of English で「英語を母（国）語として話す、話す人」という意味。たとえ英語を母国語とするネイティブスピーカーでも、have been educated in correct grammar「正しい文法の教育を受けている」とは限らないから。

\* Where 型パターン

4. **A**：Have you heard of UNICEF? It's the United Nations Children's Fund, and it tries to protect and help children all over the world.
   **B**：That kind of global effort is important.
   **A**：For that reason, I am hoping that you are willing to contribute money to UNICEF.

  **Q**：Where does UNICEF do its work?
    a. Its effort is global.　　b. In poor countries.
    c. In a certain area.　　d. Its effort is in countries at war.

解説：That kind of で「その種の、そのような」という意味。global は「世界的な、国際的な、全世界の」という意味。for that reason で「そのためにも、その理由で」という意味。willing to で「～するのをいとわない、望んでやる、快くやる」という意味。contribute は「（金・援助などを）与える、寄付する、貢献する」という意味。ユニセフのしている仕事は global effort「世界的な努力」だから。

# Part 4  Short Talks ／説明文問題

次の説明文の質問に最も適当な答えを選びなさい。

### アメリカ英語の話

The English language has many words that are borrowed from other languages. For example, in the hot months of the year, Americans relax on the *patio*, which is the area outside of the house where there is a table and chairs. This is actually a word borrowed from Spanish. They clean their hair with *shampoo*, which is a word from the Hindi language. A *kayak* is a boat in which Americans float on the river, and this word comes from the language of the Inuits, Native Americans who live in Canada. As you can see, American English has been influenced by several other languages, perhaps because the United States is such a new country, with many foreign influences.

1. From what language did American English borrow the word shampoo ?
   a. Hindi.    b. Inuit.
   c. Spanish.  d. French.

2. According to the paragraph, why are there so many borrowed words in American English?
   a. Because Americans like to speak foreign languages.
   b. Because the Native Americans taught them these words.
   c. Because it is a new country that has been influenced by many other languages.
   d. Because it is an influential country.

解説：設問1 「髪の毛を洗う」shampoo という単語は Hindi「ヒンズー語」から来たもの。borrow は「借りる」で、borrowed word だと「外来語」という意味になる。正解—(A)

設問2 本文の最後の文章にあるように、アメリカが new county「新しい国」で、many foreign influences「外国の影響が多い」から。正解—(C)

### アメリカとアフリカの歴史に貢献した Rosa Parks

Rosa Parks is one of the most influential women in African-American history. She is often referred to as "the mother of the civil rights movement," although she did not plan on it. In the 1950s, especially in the southern U.S., African-American people had to sit in the back of the bus; white people got to sit in the front. When the bus filled up, if a white person came onto the bus, black people had to give them their seats and stand. Rosa Parks, however, did not want to be treated this way. When they told her to stand up, she refused and was arrested by the police. After this happened, people protested and spoke out about the rights of African-Americans. They boycotted busses, and after more than a year, the Supreme Court of the U.S. ruled that it was against the constitution to make African-Americans sit in the back or stand on public transportation. It was a very important decision that helped give equal rights to all races in the United States.

1. Why did Rosa Parks refuse to stand up on the bus?
    - a. She was tired from work.
    - b. She had hurt her leg.
    - c. She didn't like the fact that she was being treated unfairly.
    - d. She wasn't able to stand.

2. When Rosa Parks was arrested, what did the people who were angry about it do?
    - a. Went to the jail to get her out.
    - b. Rode the bus only at night.
    - c. Stopped talking to Rosa Parks.
    - d. Protested and boycotted public transportation.

**解説**：設問1　Rosa は did not want to be treated this way「このような待遇、つまり不公平な待遇を受けるのが気に入らなかった」。正解－(B)

設問2　人びとは boycotted busses「バスをボイコット」、つまり抗議のため乗らなくなった。正解－(D)

# Part 5  Reading ／読解演習

次の段落文を読み、各設問に対して最も適切な答えを選びなさい（各段落速読問題は2分以内に終わらせなさい）。

## スピードリーディング

　Crissie cares a lot about the quality of food. She grew up in Mississippi, a state deep in the American South. The area is famous for its rich soil, which is good for farming, and Crissie's family were farmers when she was very young. They later had to give up farming when Crissie's father died and there was too much work for the rest of the family. Crissie never worked on the farm when she was young, which makes it odd that she now works in food issues as an adult.

　　1. According to the article, which thing does Crissie care about?
　　　　a. How much food there is.　　b. How good food is.
　　　　c. Whether there is food.　　　d. When food is available.

　　2. What about Mississippi makes it good for farming?
　　　　a. Air temperature.　　b. Humidity.
　　　　c. Hot springs.　　　　d. Good dirt.

　Crissie is not a farmer but an activist. She works for a group of people who try to create markets for local food. Local food is food that is grown or raised close to the place where it will be consumed. Because it doesn't have to travel very far, local food is very fresh, packed with nutrients and full of flavor. Aside from just being good food, though, local food benefits the environment by reducing gasoline consumption because it does not need to travel long distances for processing and sale.

　　1. Why is local food more nutritious than most food in supermarkets?
　　　　a. Less time passes between local food　　b. Processing enhances the flavor of
　　　　　　being picked and eaten.　　　　　　　　local food.
　　　　c. Local food requires less refrigeration.　d. Farmers who grow local food care
　　　　　　　　　　　　　　　　　　　　　　　　　　about it more.

　　2. Which of the following things does local food require less use of?
　　　　a. Money.　　　b. Oil.
　　　　c. Fertilizer.　　d. Hard work.

　Of course, local food can be bought at farmers' markets during the growing season. Almost half of the food Americans eat, however, comes from an institution like a school, hospital or restaurant. The people who prepare the food at institutions are used to buying everything from meat to fruits from a big food supplier. The advantage of this method is that it is quicker and easier to only make one order and take one delivery. Crissie and her colleagues will have to change the habits of these institutional buyers in order to create a big enough market for local food to sustain local farmers and ranchers.

1. Which of the following numbers comes closest to the amount of food Americans get from institutions?
    a. Ten percent.
    b. Twenty-five percent.
    c. Forty-five percent.
    d. Sixty-six percent.

2. What are Crissie and her colleagues working to change about institutional buyers?
    a. Stubborn attitudes.
    b. Default behaviors.
    c. Misunderstood responsibilities.
    d. Awkward presentation.

スピードリーディングで読んだものと同じ文を読みます。各設問に対して最も適切な答えを選びなさい。

### 読解問題

Crissie cares a lot about the quality of food. She grew up in Mississippi, a state deep in the American South. The area is famous for its rich soil, which is good for farming, and Crissie's family were farmers when she was very young. They later had to give up farming when Crissie's father died and there was too much work for the rest of the family. Crissie never worked on the farm when she was young, which makes it odd that she now works in food issues as an adult.

Crissie is not a farmer but an activist. She works for a group of people who try to create markets for local food. Local food is food that is grown or raised close to the place where it will be consumed. Because it doesn't have to travel very far, local food is very fresh, packed with nutrients and full of flavor. Aside from just being good food, though, local food benefits the environment by reducing gasoline consumption because it does not need to travel long distances for processing and sale.

Of course, local food can be bought at farmers' markets during the growing season. Almost half of the food Americans eat, however, comes from an institution like a school, hospital or restaurant. The people who prepare the food at institutions are used to buying everything from meat to fruits from a big food supplier. The advantage of this method is that it is quicker and easier to only make one order and take one delivery. Crissie and her colleagues will have to change the habits of these institutional buyers in order to create a big enough market for local food to sustain local farmers and ranchers.

Crissie's attachment to local food and the quality that comes with it goes deeper than her work. She makes an effort to eat local food in her home. Sometimes, that food comes from her own garden. More of the food comes from a local farm cooperative that Crissie is a member of. She pays some money at the beginning of the year and promises to work several hours on the farm. In exchange, she gets food throughout the summer and the autumn, more than enough to eat and also save up to last through the winter. In this way, Crissie ensures that her food is nutritious and benefits the people who grow it.

Comprehension Questions

1. In what field of work is Crissie involved?
    a. Government.
    b. Agriculture.
    c. Restaurant.
    d. Health.

2. Which word best describes Crissie's level of commitment to her ideals?
    a. Nonexistent.      b. Ambivalent.
    c. Aimless.          d. Zealous.

3. Who prepares much of the food that Americans eat?
    a. Family members.   b. Household servants.
    c. Institutions.     d. Farmers.

4. What does choosing to eat local food require?
    a. Strong political ideas.   b. Lifestyle changes.
    c. A large backyard.         d. A college degree.

## Part 6  Error Recognition／誤文訂正問題

各文には文法的な誤りがあります。訂正もしくは書き換えを必要とする語や語句を選びなさい。

1. I asked the <u>florist</u> to <u>delivered</u> the <u>flowers</u> on my sister's <u>birthday</u>.
   　　　　　　　A　　　　　B　　　　　　C　　　　　　　　　D
   解説：ask＋人＋不定詞で「人に〜するよう頼む」。不定詞は「to＋原形動詞」なので、過去分詞の deliveredは原形のdeliverに直されるべきである。
   正しい英文：I asked the florist to deliver the flowers on my sister's birthday.

2. Although the <u>map</u> is a <u>recent</u> one, we are unable to <u>found</u> the <u>location</u> of the convention center and hotel.
   　　　　　　　A　　　　　B　　　　　　　　　　　　　　C　　　　　　D
   解説：unableは不定詞をとる語なので、toの後に続く過去分詞形のfoundを原形のfindに直すのがこの場合正しい。
   正しい英文：Although the map is a recent one, we are unable to find the location of the convention center and hotel.

3. I have <u>decided</u> to plant low <u>growing</u> bushes in <u>front</u> of my home along the <u>foundational</u>.
   　　　　　A　　　　　　　　　　B　　　　　　　　C　　　　　　　　　　　　　D
   解説：文末がalong the foundational前置詞・冠詞・形容詞と最後が形容詞になっている。よってfoundationalを名詞のfoundation「基盤」に直すのが正解。
   正しい英文：I have decided to plant low growing bushes in front of my home along the foundation.

4. The <u>problem</u> with <u>learning</u> through <u>experience</u> is that it is often <u>pained</u>.
   　　　　A　　　　　　　　B　　　　　　　　C　　　　　　　　　　　　　　D
   解説：it is often painedは最後の過去分詞が形容詞用法なので、文法的におかしくはないが、意味が通らない。よって普通の形容詞painful「痛々しい」に置き換えることで意味が通じる。
   正しい英文：The problem with learning through experience is that it is often painful.

5. Last <u>evening</u> I watched a <u>fascinated</u> television <u>program</u> <u>featuring</u>, among other animals, the snow leopard.
   　　　　A　　　　　　　　　B　　　　　　　　　　　　C　　　　　　　D
   解説：「魅了された番組」とはいわず「魅力的な番組」としたいので、形容詞用法の過去分詞fascinatedを現在分詞のfascinatingに直す必要がある。
   正しい英文：Last evening I watched a fascinating television program featuring, among other animals, the snow leopard.

6. There is only one person in our department who has <u>accessing</u> to the vault <u>combination</u>, which makes her
   　　　　　　　　　　　　　　　　　　　　　　　　　　　　　　A　　　　　　　　　　　　B
   <u>absence</u> a <u>genuine</u> problem.
   　　C　　　　　D
   解説：access toで「〜へのアクセス」と言う意味であるが、動名詞の形でaccessing toとはいわない。よっ

　　　　て accessing を access に変える。

　　正しい英文：There is only one person in our department who has access to the vault combination, which makes her absence a genuine problem.

7. The <u>amuse</u> park has an <u>elaborate</u> <u>display</u> of fireworks every evening when it <u>closes</u>.
　　　　　A　　　　　　　　B　　　　C　　　　　　　　　　　　　　　　　D

　　解説：amusement park で「遊園地」。

　　正しい英文：The amusement park has an elaborate display of fireworks every evening when it closes.

# Part 7　Incomplete Sentence ／文法・語彙問題

文法的に適切な語や語句を1つ選び、文を完成させなさい。

1. I have taken two biology classes for six credits. Will this chemistry class _____ my science requirement?
    a. ull          b. fulfill
    c. fulfills     d. to fill

    訳：私は6単位分の2つの生物のクラスをとりました。ですからこの化学のクラスを終わらせれば、科学の必修科目を全部習得したことになりますか？
    解説：2文目の文章の述部には助動詞があるが肝心の動詞が見当たらない。よって動詞（原形）のB「成就する」が正解。

2. Even though we were _____, we could not hear each other over the pounding of the surf.
    a. yells        b. yell
    c. yelling      d. yelled

    訳：大声で叫んでいたにもかかわらず、お互いの声は打ち寄せる大波の音にかき消されてしまっていた。
    解説：従属節は意味から考えて過去進行形なので、現在文詞のCを選ぶ。

3. The film was loosely _____ on her life, but a number of artistic liberties were taken, some of them erroneous.
    a. to base      b. based
    c. bases        d. basic

    訳：その映画はおおよそ彼女の生涯をもとに作られたが、フィクションの部分も多く、中には間違ったものもある。
    解説：be based on で「～をもとにする」という表現。よってBが正解。loosely はこの場合動詞 based を修飾する副詞。

4. Most people know flowers and plants by their _____ name, for example, blue-eyed Mary, rather than their scientific name.
    a. commons      b. common
    c. commonly     d. commoner

    訳：たいていの人は、正式な学名でよりも「ブルー・アイド・メアリー」等の通称で、花や植物の名前を覚えている。
    解説：their は代名詞の所有格で、続く語は名詞になる。しかし下線部後に名詞があるので、下線はその名詞を修飾する形容詞であると考えられる。よって正解は「一般の」という意味のBになる。

5. I was up all night, ill with the flu, and called the school this morning to arrange for a _____ teacher.
    a. substituted   b. substitute
    c. substitutes   d. to substitute

    訳：インフルエンザのため昨晩は一睡もできなかったので、今朝学校に電話をし、臨時講師に授業を代行してもらうよう手配をしておいた。
    解説：冠詞と名詞の間に下線部が来ているので、下線部が文末の名詞 teacher を修飾する語であるとわかる。よって正解は形容詞のB「代理の」。

*84*

# Lesson 8 （http://audio.lincenglish.com にアクセスして音声を聞いてください）

## Part 1　Image Listening ／写真描写問題

1. 左の写真を見て、人物の行動や物の位置などについて文を 3 つ作りなさい。
   _____
   _____
   _____

2. 写真の描写文として最も適切な文を A 〜 D の中から選びなさい。
   （A），（B），（C），（D）

1. 左の写真を見て、人物の行動や物の位置などについて文を 3 つ作りなさい。
   _____
   _____
   _____

2. 写真の描写文として最も適切な文を A 〜 D の中から選びなさい。
   （A），（B），（C），（D）

1. 左の写真を見て、人物の行動や物の位置などについて文を 3 つ作りなさい。
   _____
   _____
   _____

2. 写真の描写文として最も適切な文を A 〜 D の中から選びなさい。
   （A），（B），（C），（D）

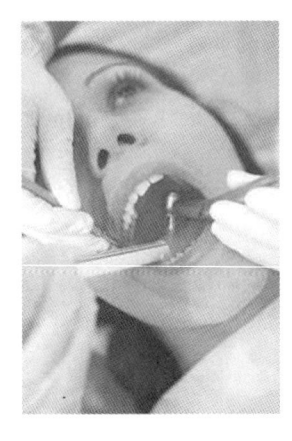

1. 左の写真を見て、人物の行動や物の位置などについて文を 3 つ作りなさい。
   _____
   _____
   _____

2. 写真の描写文として最も適切な文を A 〜 D の中から選びなさい。
   （A），（B），（C），（D）

# Part 2　Question and Response／質疑応答問題

## 重要な質問表現

What will you do with that match?
　　質問文中の with は、「(道具・手段・材料) 〜で・〜を使って」の意。

Are you anxious to graduate?
　　anxious「切望して」。類義語に eager「切望・熱望している」がある。

I had better leave early, too.
　　had better「〜したほうがいい・〜すべきだ」。この表現は「そうしないと困ったことになる」という含みをもつ。

How will you attach the ball to the stick?
　　attach A to B「A を B にくっつける・結びつける」。

Why did you quit working on that puzzle?
　　quit 〜 ing「〜することをやめる・断念する・放棄する」。

Did someone abandon that car?
　　abandon「捨てる・置き去りにする」。

When did you transfer to this school?
　　transfer「移る・転校する」。

Were you asleep when I phoned?
　　phone「電話する・電話をかける」。名詞の「電話」という意味で使われる事が多いが、ここでは動詞として使われている。

What is an appropriate way to handle a baby?
　　handle「手を触れる・手で扱う」。ここでは動詞として用いられているが、名詞の「取っ手・つまみ・ハンドル」という意味で使われることもある。

What's wrong with the computer?
　　What's wrong 〜?「何か問題でもあるのか・どうしたのか」。

## 確認ドリル

次の 1 〜 5 の質問に対して最も適切な応答をそれぞれ (A) 〜 (C) の中から選びなさい。

1. How often do you come here?
   (A)　Seldom.
   (B)　Totally.
   (C)　Properly.

2. Are you curious to know who sent the flowers?
   (A)　It is a unique opportunity.
   (B)　Absolutely. Let's open the card now.
   (C)　I can smell them already.

3. How can you concentrate on reading with all of that noise?
   (A)　I'm nearly done with my work.
   (B)　I'm able to ignore it.
   (C)　I'm afraid there has been an error.

4. Will you help me arrange my furniture?
   (A)　Yes. How much did that chair cost?
   (B)　Of course. The couch is very attractive.
   (C)　Sure. Where do you want the table?

5. Why has your income decreased?
   (A)　Because the information was required.
   (B)　Because I changed jobs.
   (C)　Because it has expanded.

## Part 3　Short Conversation ／会話問題

次の会話を聞いて、質問に最も適当な答えを選びなさい。

### 質問文パターン

\* How 型パターン

1. **A**：Your performance was a delight to see. You dance so smoothly across the stage, and you never seem nervous

   **B**：I appreciate your praise. Once I begin dancing, I'm not nervous, but before the performance I'm frightened. To calm my nerves, I stretch my muscles.

   **A**：Stretching is a creative cure for fear!

   **Q**：How does the performer get rid of her fear before the performance?
   - a. Stretches.
   - b. Nerves.
   - c. Dances.
   - d. Delights.

   解説：delight は「大喜び、歓喜、楽しみ、楽しみ（喜び）を与えるもの」という意味。praise は「賞賛、褒め言葉、ほめること、ほめられること」という意味。frightened は「怖がる、怯える」という意味。creative は「創造力のある、創造（創作、独創）的な、想像力に富んだ」という意味。cure は「治療、治療法（薬）、解決策」という意味。彼女は上演前、To calm my nerves, I stretch my muscles「落ち着くために、筋肉のストレッチをする」。

\* Why 型パターン

2. **A**：The vocabulary in this novel is too difficult for me. I need a dictionary for every page.

   **B**：Sometimes it helps to guess the meaning of an unfamiliar word by reading the words around it.

   **A**：I've tried that, but now I'm totally confused. I'll find another novel.

   **Q**：Why does the reader need another novel?
   - a. Because the words in the first novel are too difficult.
   - b. Because of the meanings of the unfamiliar words.
   - c. Because the vocabulary is too easy.
   - d. Because the first novel bored him.

   解説：vocabulary は「語彙、用語範囲、全単語、用語」という意味。unfamiliar は「未知の、なじみの薄い」という意味。totally は「まったく、完全に、すっかり」という意味。confused は「混同する、混乱する、困惑する」という意味。最初の小説は vocabulary in this novel is too difficult「語彙が難しすぎる」。

\* Which 型パターン

3. **A**：In which regions of the United States are cotton, corn, and wheat grown?

   **B**：A lot of cotton is grown in the South because it needs a mild climate. Wheat tends to be grown in the North, in states like Montana and North Dakota. Corn fields are common in the Midwest.

   **A**：I'd like to visit those regions some day.

**Q**: In which region is corn grown?

    a. North.      b. Midwest.

    c. South.      d. East.

解説：region は「地域、地方、地帯」という意味。grow は「（農作物を）栽培する、育てる、産出する」という意味。mild は「（気候が）穏やかな、温暖な」という意味。tend to be で「～する傾向がある、よく～する、～しがちである」という意味の成句。とうもろこし畑は common in the Midwest「中西部にありふれている」。

＊ What 型パターン

4. **A**：Sarah is flying to San Diego for the weekend.

   **B**：Sounds fun! Will she go to the zoo, or will she spend time on the beach? December is a great time to go whale watching, too.

   **A**：The primary reason for her trip is to visit her brother before the military sends him overseas. I doubt they will have much time to see the sights.

     **Q**：What is the primary reason for Sarah's trip to San Diego?

        a. Go to the zoo.     b. Spend time at the beach.

        c. See her brother.     d. Join the military.

解説：flying to で「飛行機で行く、飛行機を利用して旅行する」という意味。sounds ～は「～そうだ、～のようだ」という意味で使われる。primary は「第1の、主要な、最も重要な」という意味。doubt で「～かどうか疑問に思う、～でないと思う、疑わしく思う」という意味。サラがサンディエゴに行く最も重要な理由は to visit her brother before the military sends him overseas「軍が兄弟を海外へ派遣する前に訪問する」ことだから。

# Part 4　Short Talks／説明文問題

次の説明文の質問に最も適当な答えを選びなさい。

### 竜巻の威力

A tornado is a violently rotating column of air which is in contact with both a cloud base and the surface of the earth. Most intense tornadoes develop from supercells, severe thunderstorms with deep rotating updrafts. Very heavy rain, frequent lightning, strong wind gusts, and hail are common in such storms. Tornadoes can come in many shapes but are most typically in the form of a visible condensation funnel, with the narrow end touching the earth. Often, a cloud of debris encircles the lower portion of the funnel. Most tornadoes have winds of 110 mph or less, are approximately 250 feet across, and travel a few miles before dissipating. However, some tornadoes can have winds of more than 300 mph, be more than a mile across, and stay on the ground for dozens of miles. They have been observed on every continent except Antarctica. Other areas which commonly experience tornadoes include New Zealand, western and southeastern Australia, south-central Canada, northwestern and central Europe, Italy, south-central and eastern Asia, east-central South America, and Southern Africa. Most of the world's tornadoes, however, occur in the United States.

1. What is a tornado?
   a. A warm tropical storm system fueled by thunderstorms near its center.
   b. A violently rotating column of air which is in contact with a cloud base and the earth's surface.
   c. The horizontal movement of air caused by uneven heating of the earth's surface.
   d. A series of waves created when a body of water, such as an ocean, is rapidly displaced on a large scale.

2. What events commonly occur during a tornado?
   a. Dense fog.
   b. Heavy snow and blizzard conditions.
   c. Lightning, heavy rain, strong winds, and hail.
   d. Complete darkness.

解説： 設問1　本文の始めに説明があるように、violently rotating column of air「激しく回転する空気の柱」で a cloud base and the surface of the earth「雲の下部と地球の表面（地面）」に接している嵐のことである。正解－(B)

設問2　トルネード発生時によく見られるのは Very heavy rain「激しい豪雨」、frequent lightning「頻繁に走る稲妻」、strong wind gusts「強い突風」、および hai「ひょう」である。正解－(C)

### モンタナ州について

As of 2005, Montana has an estimated population of 935,670. Of that number, 16,500 are foreign-born, accounting for 1.8% of the total population. According to the 2000 U.S. Census, 1.52% of the population aged five and over speaks Spanish at home, while 1.11% speaks German. While German ancestry is the largest reported European-American ancestry in most of Montana, residents of Scandinavian ancestry are prevalent in some of the farming-dominated northern and eastern prairie regions. There are also several predominantly Native American counties, mostly around each of the seven Indian reservations. The historically mining-oriented communities of western Montana have a wider range of ethnic groups, particularly people of Eastern European and Irish-American ancestry, as well as people who originally emigrated from British mining regions such as Cornwall. Many of Montana's historic logging communities originally attracted people of Scandin-avian and Scotch-Irish descent. Montana's Hispanic population is particularly concentrated around the Billings area in south-central Montana, and the highest density of African-Americans is located in Great Falls.

1. What is the largest reported ancestry in the state of Montana?
    a. French.　　　　b. Asian.
    c. Scandinavian.　　d. German.

2. In which part of Montana do most residents of African ancestry reside?
    a. Great Falls.　　b. Missoula.
    c. Billings.　　　　d. Bozeman.

解説：設問1　本文中で紹介されているのは、ドイツ系である。正解−(D)
　　　設問2　本文最後の文がキーポイント。the highest density of African-Americans「最もアフリカ系アメリカ人が集中している場所」はビリングスである。正解−(A)

## Part 5　Reading／読解演習

次の段落文を読み、各設問に対して最も適切な答えを選びなさい（各段落速読問題は2分以内に終わらせなさい）。

### スピードリーディング

Chris has liked computers for as long as he can remember. When he was eight years old, he bought his first computer with the money from delivering newspapers. The computer was a Commodore 64, and it had less memory and computing power than a modern-day cell phone. But it was enough of a computer to teach him the basics of programming and other computer concepts.

1. How did Chris get his first computer?
   a. As a gift from his parents.
   b. By winning a contest.
   c. Saving money from his job.
   d. Inheriting it from his brother.

2. Chris's first computer is _____ by today's standards.
   a. powerful.
   b. incomplete.
   c. domestic.
   d. antiquated.

At that time, the Internet existed but Web pages were not yet something that a person could look at. Everything online was just text, and connection speeds were very slow. Sometimes, the text would come across the screen more slowly than Chris could read it. But there were discussion groups and an early form of e-mail that Chris was able to access through what were called Bulletin Board Systems. These were computers hooked up to the end of a telephone line through a modem that people could dial into.

1. What was available on the Internet at the time Chris started to use it?
   a. Web pages.
   b. Text only.
   c. Chat.
   d. Video.

2. Chris found that he could read _____ the information could get to his computer.
   a. more slowly than.
   b. as quickly as.
   c. more quickly than.
   d. only as.

Chris got to college just as the first Web pages were being created. He learned to use the first browser, called Mosaic, and started visiting Yahoo! when it was still being run by people who were in college like him. His curiosity, and a job in a computer lab, kept him involved with computers all the way through college, and his knowledge grew quite a bit. Though he never studied computers specifically, Chris became very comfortable with the principles that govern computer use.

1. When Chris first learned about the Internet, most of the users were still _____.
   a. amateurs.
   b. professionals.
   c. businesses.
   d. children.

2. What motivated Chris to learn about computers?
   a. Greed.      b. Curiosity.
   c. Comfort.    d. Knowledge.

スピードリーディングで読んだものと同じ文を読みます。各設問に対して最も適切な答えを選びなさい。

### 読解問題

Chris has liked computers for as long as he can remember. When he was eight years old, he bought his first computer with the money from delivering newspapers. The computer was a Commodore 64, and it had less memory and computing power than a modern-day cell phone. But it was enough of a computer to teach him the basics of programming and other computer concepts.

At that time, the Internet existed but Web pages were not yet something that a person could look at. Everything online was just text, and connection speeds were very slow. Sometimes, the text would come across the screen more slowly than Chris could read it. But there were discussion groups and an early form of e-mail that Chris was able to access through what were called Bulletin Board Systems. These were computers hooked up to the end of a telephone line through a modem that people could dial into.

Chris got to college just as the first Web pages were being created. He learned to use the first browser, called Mosaic, and started visiting Yahoo! when it was still being run by people who were in college like him. His curiosity, and a job in a computer lab, kept him involved with computers all the way through college, and his knowledge grew quite a bit. Though he never studied computers specifically, Chris became very comfortable with the principles that govern computer use.

When he graduated from college, Chris got a job at a company that produced mail-order catalogs. The information needed to make the catalogs was stored in large computer databases, which Chris became involved with maintaining. He became an expert in Oracle databases, one of the most popular kinds of database, and soon got a job using that knowledge. Instead of working on them directly, though, Chris became a teacher. Now he travels around the country teaching other people to administer databases.

Comprehension Questions

1. Which reason seems most likely for Chris's career success with computer technology?
   a. He is smarter than all his peers.     b. He got involved with computers at the right time.
   c. He works very hard.                    d. He has many connections in the industry.

2. What is responsible for Chris's knowledge with computers?
   a. Formal education.              b. Family instruction.
   c. His curiosity and aptitude.    d. Community job training.

3. Which of the following probably describes the way Chris would describe himself?
   a. Timid.     b. Content.
   c. Inactive.  d. Confused.

4. Which of the following would be a good title for this article?
   a. "From Hobby to Job".                   b. "Computing During the 1990s".
   c. "Catalog Company Promotes Engineer".   d. "Bulletin Board Systems and the Future".

## Part 6　Error Recognition／誤文訂正問題

各文には文法的な誤りがあります。訂正もしくは書き換えを必要とする語や語句を選びなさい。

1. My niece and I have become great friends although I wasn't aware to her existence until my brother
   　　　A　　　　　　　　　　　　　　　B　　　　　　　　　C　　　　　　　D
   passed away last year.
   - 解説：be aware of で「〜に気が付いている」という言い回し。しかし be aware to とは決して言わないので、前置詞 to を of に書き直す必要がある。
   - 正しい英文：My niece and I have become great friends although I wasn't aware of her existence until my brother passed away last year.

2. I've been thinking a lot with your idea, and there are several points I would like you to clarify.
   　　A　　　　　　　　B　　　　　　　　　　C　　　　　　　　　D
   - 解説：think about で「〜について考える」という意味なので、2つ目の下線の前置詞 with は間違い。よって、about に直すのが正解。
   - 正しい英文：I've been thinking a lot about your idea, and there are several points I would like you to clarify.

3. The cost with new cars is expected to fall as we run out of natural resources to run them.
   　　　　　A　　　　　　　　　B　　　　　　　　　C　　　　　　　D
   - 解説：新車の価格と言いたいので、前置詞は「〜にともなう」という意味の with ではなく、「〜の」という意味の of であるべき。
   - 正しい英文：The cost of new cars is expected to fall as we run out of natural resources to run them.

4. The goal with the project is to supply all of the inhabitants within a twenty mile radius of here with fresh
   　　　　A　　　　　　　B　　　　　　　　　　　　　C　　　　　　　　　　　　D
   drinking water by the end of the summer.
   - 解説：a goal of で「〜の目標」という意味。A goal with とは言わない。
   - 正しい英文：The goal of the project is to supply all of the inhabitants within a twenty mile radius of here with fresh drinking water by the end of the summer.

5. Can I to call you back in about fifteen minutes? I'm in the middle of a serious conversation.
   　A　　B　　C　　　　　　　　　　　　　　　　　　　　　D
   - 解説：助動詞 can があるので、続く動詞は原型でないとならないのに、本文では前置詞 to がついて不定詞の形になっている。よって to を外すことで文章が正しくなる。
   - 正しい英文：Can I call you back in about fifteen minutes? I'm in the middle of a serious conversation.

6. Why are you complaining? Your only household chore is to clean on your room before you go to bed.
   　　　　　A　　　　　　　　　　　　　　B　　　　　　　　C　　　　　　　　　D
   - 解説：部屋を掃除するは clean up で clean on とは言わない。よって、正しい前置詞は on ではなく up。
   - 正しい英文：Why are you complaining? Your only household chore is to clean up your room before you go to

bed.

7. It was considerate <u>of</u> my mother to <u>invited</u> all of my classmates <u>to</u> my childhood birthday parties. No one
         A     B       C
<u>ever</u> felt left out.
D

 解説：to invited は不定詞になる部分であるはずなのに、動詞が過去分詞形になっている。よって過去分詞 invited を原形の invite に直すのが正解。

 正しい英文：It was considerate of my mother to invite all of my classmates to my childhood birthday parties. No one ever felt left out.

# Part 7　Incomplete Sentence／文法・語彙問題

文法的に適切な語や語句を1つ選び、文を完成させなさい。

1. The tension _____ the feuding families could be felt as far away as the next room.
    - a. between
    - b. since
    - c. except
    - d. about

   訳：対立する家族の緊張感が隣の部屋まで伝わって来るようであった。
   解説：2つの家族の間で起こった言い争い、と言いたいので、「2者間の」と言う意味の前置詞Aが、この場合最も正しい答え。

2. One of the differences _____ primates and other mammals is the trait of opposing thumbs.
    - a. behind
    - b. across
    - c. between
    - d. except

   訳：霊長類が哺乳類との異なる1つの理由は、親指が他の4指と反対を向いている点である。
   解説：2種類の動物を引き合いに出したいので、「2者間の」と言う意味の前置詞Cが、この場合最も正しい答え。

3. With the arrival of spring, the weather conditions are genuinely improving. We should see a big change _____ the next few weeks.
    - a. for
    - b. to
    - c. over
    - d. instead

   訳：春の到来と共に、天気が回復に向かっている。ですから、2、3週間以内には天候が大幅に変わるだろうことでしょう。
   解説：BとDは訳しようがなく、Aだった場合「～の間（のみ）」になってしまうので、この場合は「～中には」と言う意味のCがもっとも内容にあてはまる。

4. He lost over ten pounds _____ his illness because he could barely even swallow.
    - a. for
    - b. by
    - c. tog
    - d. durin

   訳：彼は病気にかかっている間、食べ物を飲み込むことさえままならず、10ポンド以上も痩せてしまった。
   解説：「～の間」という期間を表す前置詞は選択肢の中ではAとDであるが、Aの場合はそれ自体で期間を表す語が来なければいけないので、この場合はあわない。よってDが最も正しい答えになる。

5. The 100 dollar bill seemed genuinely authentic except _____ the numbering in the bottom right corner.
    - a. of
    - b. to
    - c. for
    - d. in

   訳：右下の製造番号の部分を除けば、その100ドル札は本物に限りなく近いものであった。
   解説：except forで「～を除いては」と言う表現。

# Lesson 9 （http://audio.lincenglish.com にアクセスして音声を聞いてください）

## Part 1　Image Listening／写真描写問題

1. 左の写真を見て、人物の行動や物の位置などについて文を3つ作りなさい。
   _____
   _____
   _____

2. 写真の描写文として最も適切な文をA～Dの中から選びなさい。
   （A）, （B）, （C）, （D）

1. 左の写真を見て、人物の行動や物の位置などについて文を3つ作りなさい。
   _____
   _____
   _____

2. 写真の描写文として最も適切な文をA～Dの中から選びなさい。
   （A）, （B）, （C）, （D）

1. 左の写真を見て、人物の行動や物の位置などについて文を3つ作りなさい。
   _____
   _____
   _____

2. 写真の描写文として最も適切な文をA～Dの中から選びなさい。
   （A）, （B）, （C）, （D）

1. 左の写真を見て、人物の行動や物の位置などについて文を3つ作りなさい。
   _____
   _____
   _____

2. 写真の描写文として最も適切な文をA～Dの中から選びなさい。
   （A）, （B）, （C）, （D）

# Part 2　Question and Response／質疑応答問題

### 重要な質問表現

How will they promote their new product?
　　「宣伝する・販売促進する」。

Sure. I like to state my opinion.
　　（C）opinion「意見」。state an opinion で、「意見を（はっきり）述べる」の意。

Does the teacher favor one student over another?
　　favor「好む・ひいきにする」。prefer と同様「数あるもののうち1つを好むこと」という意味だが、好む対象が主に人であるという点が prefer とは異なる。

What is the opposite of positive?
　　opposite「反意語・反対の」。

Are you capable of translating this speech?
　　capable「～ができる・能力がある」。

Is he an immigrant to the United States?
　　immigrant「（外国からの）移民・移住者」。他国への移民（移出民）は emigrant。

How did he manage to recover the ball so quickly?
　　recover「（アメフトなどで）取りそこなったボールを再び確保すること」。

I'm fairly sure they will be done in an hour.
　　be fairly sure that「（主語が思うに）that 以下であるはずだ」。

How did you feel when you accomplished your goal?
　　accomplish「やり遂げる・（仕事・義務などを）遂行する」。類義語は achieve「達成する・成し遂げる」。前者には完了点が重視され、後者には努力を伴う経過に重点が置かれる。

Why did you reject his plan?
　　類義語である refuse は、断固とした、時には無礼な拒絶を意味する。reject は、さらに強くはねつけるような拒絶を意味する。

### 確認ドリル

次の 1～5 の質問に対して最も適切な応答をそれぞれ（A）～（C）の中から選びなさい。

1. Are you positive that you are right?
　　(A)　No, it's not convenient.
　　(B)　Yes, I know I'm correct.
　　(C)　Yes, they reacted quickly.

2. When will he make a decision?
　　(A)　Later today.
　　(B)　Yes, I trust him.
　　(C)　Constantly.

3. Why are you so curious about this box?
　　(A)　Because I will obtain a copy.
　　(B)　Because I don't know what it contains.
　　(C)　Because I am choosing my occupation.

4. Does she normally respond to e-mail message immediately?
　　(A)　Occasionally she receives e-mail.
　　(B)　Usually within a day or two.
　　(C)　She reads her e-mail messages closely.

5. Does the coach of the volleyball team command their respect?
   (A) Yes, the team listens to him, relying on his suggestions.
   (B) No, coaching takes a considerable amount of time, and he's very busy.
   (C) The coach is well-known and talented.

# Part 3　Short Conversation ／会話問題

次の会話を聞いて、質問に最も適当な答えを選びなさい。

> 質問文パターン

\* Why 型パターン

1.　**A**：I would like to buy a pair of shoes. They need to be practical, without high heels, and comfortable.
　　**B**：This style comes in brown and black. Would you like to try them on?
　　**A**：They look practical and they don't have high heels, but my toes hurt. May I try on that pair over there instead?

　　　　**Q**：Why did the shopper not buy the first pair of shoes?
　　　　　　a. Because she decided against buying shoes.　　b. Because they had high heels.
　　　　　　c. Because they weren't comfortable.　　d. Because they weren't the right color.

　解説：最後の話し手 A の言葉により答えは C とわかる。

\* When 型パターン

2.　**A**：We intend to finish this project within the next week. We've been working on it for about a month already.
　　**B**：You've put a lot of effort into the laboratory work.
　　**A**：Yes, that part will be done by tomorrow. We just need to complete the written report.

　　　　**Q**：When do they intend to complete the project?
　　　　　　a. Sooner or later.　　b. About a month.
　　　　　　c. By tomorrow.　　d. Within the next week.

　解説：最初の文で「来週中に」と言っている。

\* Where 型パターン

3.　**A**：I heard that last night someone robbed the grocery store across the street.
　　**B**：Yes, the police pursued the thief onto the path along the river, but he escaped.
　　**A**：I wonder if the police are still searching for him. I'd look downtown near the library.

　　　　**Q**：Where did the police chase the thief?
　　　　　　a. Downtown.　　b. Near the library.
　　　　　　c. Across the street.　　d. Along the river.

　解説：along the river は「川沿い」という意味。

\* Who 型パターン

4. **A**：I'm working for two hours a week in a special recreation program for the elderly.

   **B**：The activities must be very different from those you would use for a youth group or for college students.

   **A**：No, the activities are similar. The speed at which the activities are done is slower.

   **Q**：For whom are the activities done more slowly?
   - a. People recovering from illness.
   - b. College students.
   - c. Youth.
   - d. Older people.

   **解説**：elderly は「年配の」という意味。

# Part 4　Short Talks／説明文問題

次の説明文の質問に最も適当な答えを選びなさい。

### 大統領選挙

Presidents and Vice Presidents of the United States are elected every four years. They are elected indirectly through the United States Electoral College. The Presidential Office is the only nationally-elected office in the United States. On Election Day, the voting citizens select their preferred candidate, usually by voting for a slate of electors put forward by the candidate's party. The ballots for each voting citizen typically have the names of the candidates for President and Vice President (running together on a ticket), and votes for those individuals translate at the state level into votes for the electors chosen from their respective parties. In December, following the general election, electors gather at their respective state capitals to cast their ballots, which are then transmitted to Congress under the care of the sitting Vice President of the United States. Each elector casts one vote for President and one vote for Vice President. The ballots are counted and certified in January before both houses of Congress. If a candidate for President or Vice President fails to achieve a majority of votes, the United States House of Representatives (voting by state) chooses the next President from among the candidates. The United States Senate (voting normally) chooses the Vice President.

1. How are the President and Vice President of the United States elected to office under normal circumstances?

    a. They must obtain a majority of votes from all voting precincts in the fifty States.
    b. The President is appointed by the United States House of Representatives, and the Vice President is appointed by the United States Senate.
    c. They campaign in the largest U.S. cities and collect votes from the citizens United as they they travel from state to state.
    d. They are elected indirectly through the United States Electoral College.

2. Which other offices are elected by means of a national election?

    a. State Governors.　　b. Congressmen.
    c. State Representatives.　　d. None of the above.

解説：設問1　キーポイントは indirectly through the United States Electoral College アメリカ合衆国大統領・副大統領選挙人団によって間接的に選ばれるということ。正解－(D)

設問2　アメリカで唯一全国的に選ばれる団は大統領および副大統領を選挙する the United States Electoral College「大統領・副大統領選挙人団」である。正解－(D)

### アルマジロの話

Armadillos are prolific diggers. Many species use their sharp claws for digging and finding food, as well as for making their dens. The diet of different armadillo species varies but consists mainly of insects, grubs and other invertebrates. Some species, however, feed mainly on ants. Armadillos have poor vision but are not blind. The armor is formed by plates of dermal bone covered in small, overlapping scales called scutes. This armor-like skin appears to be the main defense of many armadillos, although most will try to escape predators by fleeing or digging their way to safety. Some armadillos when threatened by a predator will roll up into a ball. Other armadillo species cannot roll up because they have too many plates, but instead will jump straight up into the air when surprised. Armadillos have short legs but can move quickly. Because of the weight of their armor, armadillos will sink in water, but they have the ability to remain underwater for as long as six minutes.

1. The armor of an armadillo is formed by what?
    a. Hard shells formed by healing and calcification of injuries from predator attacks.
    b. Bones in their spinal columns which they can eject when threatened.
    c. Dermal bone covered in scales, or scutes.
    d. A shell or hard cover similar to a to rtoise shell.

2. What do armadillos use their claws for?
    a. Digging and foraging for food; building their dens.
    b. Fighting off predators.
    c. Building protective stockades around their dens.
    d. Removing parasites from their scutes.

解説：設問1　キーポイントは by plates of dermal bone covered in scutes スキューツと呼ばれるもので覆われた骨のように堅い皮膚の板の部分。正解－(C)

設問2　キーポイントは本文1文目の、Armadillos are prolific diggers アルマジロがとてもよく穴を掘るということ。正解－(A)

# Part 5 Reading／読解演習

次の段落文を読み、各設問に対して最も適切な答えを選びなさい（各段落速読問題は2分以内に終わらせなさい）。

### スピードリーディング

Roy describes his lifestyle by saying, "I never fired my drummer." Roy's remark refers to an old adage that describes an independent person as "marching to the beat of his own drummer." What Roy means is that most of the people he knew when he was young have chosen lives without much challenge or originality. That is not what Roy has chosen.

1. "Marching to the beat of his own drummer" is what kind of saying?
   a. Interjection.     b. Maxim.
   c. Eulogy.          d. Occupationo.

2. Which of the following best describes Roy's character?
   a. Argumentative.   b. Boring.
   c. Free spirit.     d. Ambitious.

Any story about Roy must be prefaced by something like "the last time I saw Roy" because what Roy does seems to vary quite a bit from month to month. Roy is searching for something, maybe a life that allows him to be creative, maybe just for somewhere comfortable that's not confining. Whatever he is looking for, Roy has yet to find it. Along the way, though, Roy visits a lot of interesting places.

1. While Roy would not mind a comfortable life, he is concerned about feeling _____.
   a. roped.           b. gentle.
   c. trapped.         d. aimless.

2. At the time of the story, which of the following best describes Roy's status?
   a. Enthusiastic.    b. Still searching.
   c. Angry.           d. Settled.

Most recently, Roy just returned from a stint working on a fishing boat off the coast of Alaska. He spent at least eight hours a day moving boxes of frozen fish in a floating warehouse. It was hard work but the kind that leaves Roy's mind free to go where it pleases and that's what matters most to him. Roy is determined that he is going to get paid to use his brain as he pleases. Short of that, he'll use his back to earn enough to live.

1. Where did Roy's job in Alaska take place?
   a. In an office.    b. Outdoors.
   c. On a boat.       d. In a truck.

2. Which of the following best describes the sort of work Roy was doing in Alaska?
   a. Manual labor.    b. Fishing.
   c. Management.    d. Creative arts.

スピードリーディングで読んだものと同じ文を読みます。各設問に対して最も適切な答えを選びなさい。

### 読解問題

Roy describes his lifestyle by saying, "I never fired my drummer." Roy's remark refers to an old adage that describes an independent person as "marching to the beat of his own drummer." What Roy means is that most of the people he knew when he was young have chosen lives without much challenge or originality. That is not what Roy has chosen.

Any story about Roy must be prefaced by something like "the last time I saw Roy" because what Roy does seems to vary quite a bit from month to month. Roy is searching for something, maybe a life that allows him to be creative, maybe just for somewhere comfortable that's not confining. Whatever he is looking for, Roy has yet to find it. Along the way, though, Roy visits a lot of interesting places.

Most recently, Roy just returned from a stint working on a fishing boat off the coast of Alaska. He spent at least eight hours a day moving boxes of frozen fish in a floating warehouse. It was hard work but the kind that leaves Roy's mind free to go where it pleases and that's what matters most to him. Roy is determined that he is going to get paid to use his brain as he pleases. Short of that, he'll use his back to earn enough to live.

One attempt that Roy has made at making a living from doing what he pleases with his talent was stand-up comedy. Having experienced some success with getting up in front of a crowd and telling jokes in the small Midwestern city where he lived, Roy decided to move to Los Angeles, California, and try to break into a bigger market. Roy did not like the city and how much money it took for him to live there. He left and took that job in Alaska, but it's only seasonal work. That means Roy has plenty of time to do what he likes, moving from place to place, collecting stories and leaving them behind for the people he visits as he goes.

Comprehension Questions

1. Which of the following best describes the type of article you have just read?
   a. Interview.    b. Profile.
   c. Editorial.    d. Scenery.

2. Which word best describes Roy's character as described in the article?
   a. Unremarkable.    b. Tidy.
   c. Eccentric.    d. Fashionable.

3. Which of the following seems most important to Roy?
   a. Financial success.    b. Creative freedom.
   c. Family connections.    d. Education.

4. What would be the best title for this article?
   a. "Working for a Living"    b. "Aiming to Succeed"
   c. "Searching for Satisfaction"    d. "Comedy in Alaska"

## Part 6　Error Recognition／誤文訂正問題

各文には文法的な誤りがあります。訂正もしくは書き換えを必要とする語や語句を選びなさい。

1. Her descriptive of the investment opportunities at my local bank made me want to look into them.
　　　　 A　　　　　　　　　　　　　B　　　　　　　　　　　　 C　　　 D

    解説：herは代名詞の所有格で、名詞が続かないといけないのに、本文ではdescriptiveと形容詞が来ている。よってdescriptiveを名詞のdescriptionに書き変える。

    正しい英文：Her description of the investment opportunities at my local bank made me want to look into them.

2. We had a lot of fun to watch the comedian imitate various political figures.
　　　 A　　　　　　 B　　　　　　　　　 C　　　　　 D

    解説：have fun ＋動名詞で「～して楽しむ」という熟語。しかし同じ名詞形の不定詞には置き換えられない。よって2つ目の下線をwatchingに直す。

    正しい英文：We had a lot of fun watching the comedian imitate various political figures.

3. The banker sit in the vault weighing gold bricks for the upcoming shipment to Denver.
　　　　　　 A　　　　　　　 B　　　　　　　　 C　　 D

    解説：2つ目の下線で「量っている」と進行形が使われているので、1つ目の動詞も時制を合わせ、進行形のis sittingに直す。

    正しい英文：The banker is sitting in the vault weighing gold bricks for the upcoming shipment to Denver.

4. The children spent several hours hunt for the treasure, which turned out to be less interesting than they
　　　　　　　 A　　　　　　　　 B　　　　　　　　　　　　　 C　　　　　　　　　　 D
had imagined.

    解説：spend time ＋動名詞で「～に時間を費やす」という表現。よって文中の現在形は間違い。huntはhuntingでないといけない。

    正しい英文：The children spent several hours hunting for the treasure, which turned out to be less interesting than they had imagined.

5. She sat at the table whetting her appetite for the six-course meal for follow.
　　　　 A　　　　　　　　 B　　　　 C　　　　　　　　　　　　　　 D

    解説：meal to followで「出てくる食事」という表現。meal for followは文法的には意味的にもおかしいので、前置詞forは間違いである。

    正しい英文：She sat at the table whetting her appetite for the six-course meal to follow.

6. "Have you had any problems in your new neighborhood?" "No, but I do seem to have a problem to make
　　　　　　 A　　　　　　　　　　　　　　　　　　　　　　　　　　　　　　 B　　　　　　　　　 C
friends."

    解説：have a problem ＋動名詞で「～する問題がある」という表現。よって最後の下線部の不定詞を動名詞のhavingに書き直す。

正しい英文："Have you had any problems in your new neighborhood?" "No, but I do seem to have a problem making friends."

7. My husband <u>finds</u> two elk antlers <u>lying</u> near a trail he <u>took</u> while <u>hunting</u> last weekend.
       A       B      C    D

解説：last weekend と明らかに過去の話をしているにもかかわらず、動詞が現在形の finds ままである。よって finds は過去形の found に直されるべきである。

正しい英文：My husband found two elk antlers lying near a trail he took while hunting last weekend.

# Part 7  Incomplete Sentence ／文法・語彙問題

文法的に適切な語や語句を 1 つ選び、文を完成させなさい。

1. You don't want to be a participant in the spacecraft research? I can't understand _____ not wanting to do this.
   - a. you're
   - b. your
   - c. you
   - d. yours

   訳：宇宙船のリサーチに参加したくないという訳ですか？　あなたがやりたくないなんて信じられません。
   解説：not wantingは動名詞の否定形で、名詞句扱いである。よって代名詞の所有格yourが正しい答えになる。

2. Helping people learn how _____ their prejudices is a rewarding experience.
   - a. to overcame
   - b. overcome
   - c. overcame
   - d. to overcome

   訳：先入観をいかに克服するかを人びとに教えるのはとてもやりがいのある経験です。
   解説：how toで「～の仕方」という表現。to以降は不定詞であることに注意する。

3. My mother opened the oven _____ the cake she had prepared for dessert.
   - a. removed
   - b. to remove
   - c. for removing
   - d. removes

   訳：デザートに用意しておいたケーキを取り出すために、母親はオーブンを開けた。
   解説：remove「取りだす」ために「オーブンを開け」ようとしているので、この場合は不定詞の副詞用法「～のために」がもっとも当てはまる。よって正解はBのto remove。

4. There is absolutely no trick to _____ a good artist. You only have to follow your natural instinct.
   - a. being
   - b. be
   - c. to be
   - d. been

   訳：立派なアーティストになるのにトリックなどありませんよ。ただ自分の本能に従えばよいのです。
   解説：no trick to＋名詞句で「～の仕掛けはない」という表現。前置詞toがあるため、不定詞と考えがちだが、この場合は動名詞が正解。

5. Do you see the business _____ any income? If not, it's time to do something different.
   - a. generating
   - b. generated
   - c. to generate
   - d. as generated

   訳：そのビジネスは利益を生んでいますか？　そうでなければ、何か違うことをすべきです。
   解説：see＋人・物＋現在分詞で「(人・物)が～しているのを目にする」。よってAが正解。

# Lesson 10 （http://audio.lincenglish.com にアクセスして音声を聞いてください）

## Part 1　Image Listening／写真描写問題

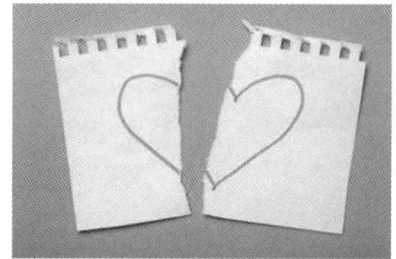

1. 左の写真を見て、人物の行動や物の位置などについて文を3つ作りなさい。
   _____
   _____
   _____

2. 写真の描写文として最も適切な文をA～Dの中から選びなさい。
   （A），（B），（C），（D）

1. 左の写真を見て、人物の行動や物の位置などについて文を3つ作りなさい。
   _____
   _____
   _____

2. 写真の描写文として最も適切な文をA～Dの中から選びなさい。
   （A），（B），（C），（D）

1. 左の写真を見て、人物の行動や物の位置などについて文を3つ作りなさい。
   _____
   _____
   _____

2. 写真の描写文として最も適切な文をA～Dの中から選びなさい。
   （A），（B），（C），（D）

1. 左の写真を見て、人物の行動や物の位置などについて文を3つ作りなさい。
   _____
   _____
   _____

2. 写真の描写文として最も適切な文をA～Dの中から選びなさい。
   （A），（B），（C），（D）

# Part 2  Question and Response／質疑応答問題

### 重要な質問表現

What occasion are you celebrating?
　　occasion「出来事・特別な行事」。ある特定の目的や主旨を含んだ場面を意味する。
What do you think accounts for the popularity of that politician?
　　account for「（事の理由・原因を）説明する・〜の原因となる」。
Does the dog obey its master?
　　obey「（人）の言うことを聞く・服従する」。
What part of the body is primarily responsible for tasting flavors of food?
　　responsible for「〜に関与する・〜に対して責任がある」。
What are you going to do about your debt?
　　debt「借金・負債」。
Has he warned you about the recent virus?
　　warn「警告する」。危険・不利な事態などを避けさせるために注意・警告などを与えるという意味。
Was the ticket agent able to help you?
　　agent「代理業者・代行者」。agency は代理業務とそれが行われる場所を指すが、agent は人に重点が置かれる。
My hands are so cold. What can I do to warm them up?
　　warm up「暖める」。
He was anxious to get to the party on time.
　　anxious to「〜することを切望する」。
The passengers are standing in a line.
　　stand in line「行列を作る・列に並ぶ」。

### 確認ドリル

次の1〜5の質問に対して最も適切な応答をそれぞれ（A）〜（C）の中から選びなさい。

1. Did he abandon his attempt to solve the mystery?
   (A) He will read the novel because it's a mystery.
   (B) He quit trying yesterday.
   (C) The statement was delivered on time.

2. Why do they oppose the plan?
   (A) Because the address is the same.
   (B) Because he is a genius.
   (C) Because it's a threat to their job.

3. Why is he handling the cords under his computer?
   (A) Because it's a tradition.
   (B) Because the computer can be an educational tool.
   (C) Because he's having technical problems with his computer.

4. How would you like to divide the money?
   (A) Unfortunately.
   (B) Fairly.
   (C) Valuable.

5. Why did he rush his roommate?
   (A) Because he greets everyone in such a friendly manner.
   (B) Because of the enormous amount of work.
   (C) Because he was anxious to get to the party on time.

# Part 3　Short Conversation／会話問題

次の会話を聞いて、質問に最も適当な答えを選びなさい。

## 質問文パターン

\* What 型パターン

1. **A**：Look at those two groups of children. They're pretending to be soldiers.
   **B**：The tall boy near the tree seems to be in command of his group. He just ordered them to surround the others.
   **A**：It is said that a natural leader will evolve from a group as it works together.

   **Q**：What are the children pretending?
   　　　a. Where to surround others.　　b. To be soldiers.
   　　　c. How to choose a leader.　　　d. To work together.

   解説：pretend「～のふりをする」。

\* How 型パターン

2. **A**：Madeline is so kind. After I lost the race, she made me feel confident and eager to try again.
   **B**：She does have a positive viewpoint.
   **A**：Also, she's a genius at choosing the right words for every situation.

   **Q**：How does Madeline help her friends?
   　　　a. Helps win a race.　　　　　b. Says the right thing.
   　　　c. Will always try again.　　　d. She's a genius.

   解説：genius「天才」。

\* Why 型パターン

3. **A**：Why did you read the first two pages of this novel aloud to the class?
   **B**：I hoped to stimulate their interest in the story.
   **A**：It seems to have worked. The room is silent, and all of the students are eagerly reading their own copy of the novel.

   **Q**：Why did the teacher read the first two pages aloud to the class?
   　　　a. To teach students to read.　　　　b. To create a silent class room.
   　　　c. To stimulate interest in the novel.　　d. To help students understand the novel.

   解説：stimulate「刺激する」。

\* Which 型パターン

4. **A**：Jacob is taking me out to dinner tonight.
   **B**：What's the special occasion?
   **A**：He has just been hired to work in the medical research laboratory. The experience will be valuable to his career, and he'll be earning more money, too.

   **Q**：Which experience will be valuable to Jacob's career?
      a. Going out to dinner.    b. The special occasion.
      c. Working in a laboratory.    d. Earning money.

解説：The experience「その経験」は医療研究室で働くことを指している。

## Part 4　Short Talks／説明文問題

次の説明文の質問に最も適当な答えを選びなさい。

### クリストファー・コロンバス

Around 1492, when Christopher Columbus sailed, most of the inhabitants of the Americas lived in Mexico. At that time, the city of Tenochtitlan was one of the biggest cities in the world. When people from Spain arrived in the area and settled there, they brought with them many diseases, including smallpox. Over 90% of the population died as a result. The population slowly grew over the next few centuries, and when Mexico became more industrialized, the population grew even more quickly. Today, there are about 94 million people who live in all of Mexico. The increase in population and industry has, however, had a negative impact on the county's natural resources and people. The forests are disappearing, and there is so much pollution that Mexico City has one of the worst air-quality problems in the world. The economy is also very poor, with many people living in poverty. Despite its problems, Mexico continues to be a beautiful country with kind, hard-working people.

1. What caused over 90% of the population to die when the Spaniards arrived?
   a. Smallpox and other diseases.　　b. Civil wars.
   c. A large earthquake.　　d. Bad air quality.

2. What are two of Mexico's biggest problems today?
   a. There are not enough people to fill all of the jobs.
   b. The economy and environmental quality are not good.
   c. The population is too small.
   d. The forests are taking over the cities.

解説：設問1　Spaniard「スペイン人」がやって来たとき、small－poxをはじめとした多くの病気を治した。正解－(A)

設問2　今日メキシコシティで問題となっているのは、so much pollution「多くの公害」とThe economy is also very poor「経済が貧しい」ということである。正解－(B)

### アボガド

Avocados are green fruits that grow on trees in warm climates. They have a rough, dark-green skin and a smooth, creamy interior that tastes a bit like a nut. The center of an avocado contains a large seed, called the pit. When people eat an avocado, they can save this pit and grow an avocado plant from it. Avocados are very healthy, containing many important vitamins and minerals. They have 60% more potassium than bananas do, which is an important mineral for the muscles and electrolyte balance in the body. Although it contains more fat than other fruits, it is a healthy kind of fat, good for the skin and hair. Best of all, avocados taste terrific! People around the world put them in salads and on sandwiches, and use them for a variety of other meals. In Japanese cuisine, avocados are one ingredient in California rolls. Avocados are my favorite fruit in the world!

1. What can you do with an avocado pit?
    a. Gain extra nutrition.           b. Grow a plant from it.
    c. Nothing; you should throw it away.    d. Grind it up to make nuts.

2. What mineral is found more in avocados than bananas?
    a. Vitamins and minerals.    b. Potassium.
    c. Sodium.                   d. A pit.

解説：設問1　Rough, dark green skin「ざらざらとした深緑の皮」と、creamy で nut のような味の中身のアボカドの center「中心部」にある種は、採っておけば後で苗木を育てることができる。正解 − (B)

設問2　アボカドに含まれている mineral で本文中紹介されているのは potassium カリウムで、Banana との比較がされている。正解 − (B)

## Part 5　Reading／読解演習

次の段落文を読み、各設問に対して最も適切な答えを選びなさい（各段落速読問題は2分以内に終わらせなさい）。

### スピードリーディング

　Polebridge is a small town in northern Montana. There are only two ways into and out of town: the road that runs past the only buildings in town. In one direction, the road goes north to Canada; the border is about thirty kilometers away. The other exit points south toward the small cities in Montana's Flathead Valley. Neither way is paved and there is no electricity coming into town from either direction.

  1. What is located directly north of Polebridge?
    a. Canadian border.  b. Flathead Valley.
    c. Montana.  d. Glacier National Park.

  2. How many roads run through Polebridge?
    a. Zero.  b. One.
    c. Two.  d. Four.

　During the summer, Polebridge is a haven for tourists. The edge of Glacier National Park is walking distance from the center of town. Glacier National Park is an enormous expanse of the some of the most beautiful and treacherous mountain terrain in Montana. In the summer, Glacier attracts thousands of people from all over the world. Of these visitors, only a small number visit Polebridge but, since Polebridge is so small, their presence makes a huge difference.

  1. Which of the following best describes Polebridge in the summer time?
    a. Manufacturing center.  b. Logging town.
    c. Trading post.  d. Vacation destination.

  2. Which term best describes the terrain in Glacier National Park?
    a. Prairie.  b. Marine.
    c. Alpine.  d. Hilly.

　There are only a few places for a visitor to Polebridge to go. There is a small store called Polebridge Mercantile that sells food, batteries and other things that people might need to buy. The Mercantile is also a bakery, generally agreed to be the best for hundreds of miles, and people sometimes travel long distances just to have a muffin or pastry. Aside from the Mercantile, there is only one other business, a restaurant and bar run by the daughter of the couple who owns the Mercantile.

  1. What is the Polebridge Mercantile famous for?
    a. Music.  b. Scenery.
    c. Bakery.  d. Hospitality.

2. How are the people who run the Mercantile related to the person who runs Polebridge's only restaurant?

  a. They are her children.  b. They are her parents.

  c. They are lifelong friends.  d. They do not get along.

スピードリーディングで読んだものと同じ文を読みます。各設問に対して最も適切な答えを選びなさい。

### 読解問題

 Polebridge is a small town in northern Montana. There are only two ways into and out of town: the road that runs past the only buildings in town. In one direction, the road goes north to Canada; the border is about thirty kilometers away. The other exit points south toward the small cities in Montana's Flathead Valley. Neither way is paved and there is no electricity coming into town from either direction.

 During the summer, Polebridge is a haven for tourists. The edge of Glacier National Park is walking distance from the center of town. Glacier National Park is an enormous expanse of the some of the most beautiful and treacherous mountain terrain in Montana. In the summer, Glacier attracts thousands of people from all over the world. Of these visitors, only a small number visit Polebridge but, since Polebridge is so small, their presence makes a huge difference.

 There are only a few places for a visitor to Polebridge to go. There is a small store called Polebridge Mercantile that sells food, batteries and other things that people might need to buy. The Mercantile is also a bakery, generally agreed to be the best for hundreds of miles, and people sometimes travel long distances just to have a muffin or pastry. Aside from the Mercantile, there is only one other business, a restaurant and bar run by the daughter of the couple who owns the Mercantile.

 In total, there are only ten permanent residents of Polebridge. When the tourist season ends in the fall, it becomes a very quiet place to live. Visitors from out of town still sometimes come to stay in a cabin and cross-country ski nearby. Mostly, though, people in Polebridge chop wood to keep their stoves going and then burn the wood to keep warm. They play music and read and occasionally go into town. But it's a lot quieter in Polebridge than in the nearby towns, and people who live in Polebridge prefer it that way.

Comprehension Questions

 1. Which word best describes Polebridge?
  a. Rural.  b. Exurban.
  c. Suburban.  d. Urban.

 2. Because Polebridge is far from other places, it could be considered _____.
  a. pointed.  b. remote.
  c. summery.  d. hermetic.

 3. What is Polebridge's main industry?
  a. Technology.  b. Music production.
  c. Tourism.  d. Logging.

 4. Which of the following would affect Polebridge most?
  a. An increase in gasoline prices.  b. The opening of the Canadian border.
  c. Development in the Flathead Valley.  d. The closing of Glacier National Park.

# Part 6  Error Recognition／誤文訂正問題

各文には文法的な誤りがあります。訂正もしくは書き換えを必要とする語や語句を選びなさい。

1. The emperor's penguin, the largest of all penguins, is an <u>inhabitant</u> of Antarctica. Though <u>clumsy</u> on ice,
   　　　　　　　　　　　　　　　　　　　　　　　　　　　　　A 　　　　　　　　　　　　　　B
   it has great <u>agility</u> in water.
   　　　　　　　　C
   - 解説：The emperor penguin で「コウテイペンギン」。The emperor's penguin だと「皇帝のペンギン」とおかしくなる。
   - 正しい英文：The emperor penguin, the largest of all penguins, is an inhabitant of Antarctica. Though clumsy on ice, it has great agility in water.

2. We <u>traced</u> the <u>owner</u> of the car through the registration we <u>found</u> in the glove compartment. The car was
   　　　A 　　　　B 　　　　　　　　　　　　　　　　　　　　　　　C
   <u>definite</u> stolen.
   　　D
   - 解説：最後の下線部が形容詞であるが、最後の語もまた形容詞である。下線部が形容詞を修飾するには副詞でないといけないので、definite を definitely に直す必要がある。
   - 正しい英文：We traced the owner of the car through the registration we found in the glove compartment. The car was definitely stolen.

3. The <u>explosion</u> of the water heater was the <u>ultimate</u> demise of the old dwelling. We <u>board</u> up the building
   　　　A 　　　　　　　　　　　　　　　　　　B 　　　　　　　　　　　　　　　　　　　　　　　　　C
   so no one could <u>access</u> it.
   　　　　　　　　　D
   - 解説：1文目のwasで過去形を表しているので、2文目も時制を合わせる必要がある。よってboardを過去形のboardedに直す必要がある。
   - 正しい英文：The explosion of the water heater was the ultimate demise of the old dwelling. We boarded up the building so no one could access it.

4. I <u>found</u> no <u>spare</u> in my trunk when I <u>proceeded</u> to change my flat tire. To say that I was <u>profound</u> annoyed
   　　A 　　　　B 　　　　　　　　　　　　　　C 　　　　　　　　　　　　　　　　　　　　　　　　　　D
   is an understatement.
   - 解説：最後の下線が形容詞 annoyed を修飾しようとしているのに、形容詞なので、副詞に直さないと文法的におかしい。よって profound を profoundly に直す必要がある。
   - 正しい英文：I found no spare in my trunk when I proceeded to change my flat tire. To say that I was profoundly annoyed is an understatement.

5. <u>Unlike</u> as it may seem, my white neighbor who was raised in a racially <u>prejudiced</u> environment is soon
   　　A 　　　　　　　　　　　　　　　　　　　　　　　　　　　　　　　　　　B

to marry Harry, a black co-worker, who has an equally racially charged background.
                                             C                    D

  解説：Unlikely as it may seem で意外なことかもしれないがという表現。
  正しい英文：Unlikely as it may seem, my white neighbor who was raised in a racially prejudiced environment is soon to marry Harry, a black co-worker, who has an equally racially charged background.


6. When the product failed to perform as promised, management offered to substituted it with a similar,
              A                                                        B                 C
   but not identical, item.
           D

   解説：offer to の前置詞 to は不定詞なので、続く動詞は原形動詞でないといけない。よって過去分詞 substituted は substitute に直されないといけない。
   正しい英文：When the product failed to perform as promised, management offered to substitute it with a similar, but not identical, item.


7. The young woman chose to make a public profession of faith by joining a spirit order of women, the Sisters
                    A                    B                              C
   of Charity, who minister to the dying.
                   D

   解説：spirit order が名詞・名詞でおかしい。よって最初の名詞が後方の名詞を修飾する形容詞でないといけない。よって spirit を spiritual に直す。
   正しい英文：The young woman chose to make a public profession of faith by joining a spiritual order of women, the Sisters of Charity, who minister to the dying.

# Part 7  Incomplete Sentence ／文法・語彙問題

文法的に適切な語や語句を1つ選び、文を完成させなさい。

1. As with numerous Christian families, our family _____ gathers at Easter for celebration and an egg hunt for the children.

    a. traditions	b. traditional
    c. traditionally	d. tradition

    訳：他のクリスチャンの家族と同様に、私たち家族もイースターには集まって食事をし、子供のためにエッグハントをします。

    解説：family tradition で「家族の伝統」という表現がこの場合は下線部が動詞の gathers を修飾しているので、副詞の traditionally でないといけない。よって正解は C。（注釈：as with「〜と同様に」）

2. I always thought he was a passive child, so I was quite astonished at his _____ playing on the soccer field.

    a. aggress	b. aggressive
    c. aggression	d. being aggressive

    訳：私はいつも彼が消極的な子だと思っていました。ですから、サッカー彼が押しの強いプレーをするのを見て非常に驚きました。

    解説：代名詞所有格の his と名詞の playing に狭まれているので、名詞を修飾できる形容詞が下線部に来ることがわかる。よって形容詞 aggressive「攻撃的な」がこの場合あてはまる。よって正解は B。

3. I found his perspective on the issue of immigration _____ but confusing, especially in consideration of his family's political background and national heritage.

    a. fascination	b. fascinate
    c. fascinating	d. fascinates

    訳：彼の移民に対する見解は非常に興味深いものであり、また同時に混乱させる内容であった。彼の家族の政治的背景と国の伝統について考えると、特にそうであった。

    解説：S＋V＋O＋C の第5文型であり、下線部と confusing は補語になる。下線部は confusing に形を合わせ、形容詞でないといけないので、この場合は選択肢の C がもっとも正しい形となる。

4. The fire marshal determined the fire was _____ set; consequently, the matter will be further investigated by law enforcement.

    a. deliberated	b. deliberately
    c. deliberate	d. deliberates

    訳：消防所長はその火災が人為的であったと結論付けた。よって、法の下に調査が進められる予定です。

    解説：was set は過去受動態で「設定された」という意味で、下線がその間にあることから、その語が動詞を修飾する副詞であるとわかる。よって副詞の B の「わざと」が正しい答え。

5. The participant from Kenya burst Jim's bubble when, in _____ of an eye, the Kenyan crossed the finish line in front of Jim and won the race.

   a. the blink  b. to blink
   c. blink   d. blinked

訳：ジムの夢は、ケニア出身の選手が目前でゴールの紐を断ち切った瞬間に壊されてしまった。

解説：in the blink of an eye で「一瞬の間」という表現なので、A が答えになる。文中に出てくる burst one's bubble は「〜の夢が壊される」という意味。

# Lesson 11 (http://audio.lincenglish.com にアクセスして音声を聞いてください)

## Part 1　Image Listening ／写真描写問題

1. 左の写真を見て、人物の行動や物の位置などについて文を 3 つ作りなさい。
   _____
   _____
   _____

2. 写真の描写文として最も適切な文を A ～ D の中から選びなさい。
   （A），（B），（C），（D）

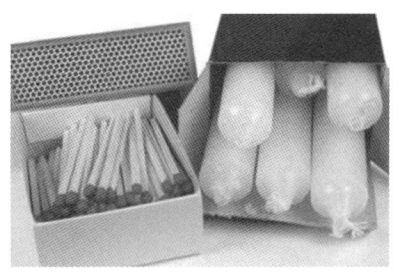

1. 左の写真を見て、人物の行動や物の位置などについて文を 3 つ作りなさい。
   _____
   _____
   _____

2. 写真の描写文として最も適切な文を A ～ D の中から選びなさい。
   （A），（B），（C），（D）

1. 左の写真を見て、人物の行動や物の位置などについて文を 3 つ作りなさい。
   _____
   _____
   _____

2. 写真の描写文として最も適切な文を A ～ D の中から選びなさい。
   （A），（B），（C），（D）

1. 左の写真を見て、人物の行動や物の位置などについて文を 3 つ作りなさい。
   _____
   _____
   _____

2. 写真の描写文として最も適切な文を A ～ D の中から選びなさい。
   （A），（B），（C），（D）

# Part 2　Question and Response／質疑応答問題

## 重要な質問表現

May I give you a piece of advice?
　　　a piece of advice「ひとつの忠告」。
Why was she examining the ring?
　　　examine「(詳細に〜を) 観察する・調べる」。
He wanted to complete the job.
　　　complete the job「その仕事を完成する・やり遂げる」。
Would you agree that Professor Blum is an authority on physics?
　　　authority「権威・権力」。
What is the advantage of exporting our product?
　　　advantage「有利な点・利点」。反義語は disadvantage「不利・不都合」。
I have the whole afternoon.
　　　whole「すべての・全部の・総」。欠けた部分のない全体を強調する語。
Did the music company release your song yet?
　　　release「(CDや本などを) 発売する・売り出す」。
I'm tired of a week of rain. Is a significant change in the weather predicted?
　　　predict「予報・予測する」。科学的な推論に基づく予測を意味することが多いが、軽い予想にも用いられる。
For what distinction was the soldier recommended?
　　　distinction「勲章・栄誉の印」。
I persuaded them to cooperate.
　　　persuade「説得する・説き伏せる」。

## 確認ドリル

次の1〜5の質問に対して最も適切な応答をそれぞれ (A)〜(C) の中から選びなさい。

1. Do you have any questions about the grammar lesson?
   (A)　No, I think I understand the structure you explained.
   (B)　I still don't quite understand the rules for basketball.
   (C)　Yes, when did the revolution in Russia begin?

2. What do you intend to call your new dog?
   (A)　Yes, I'll call you tomorrow.
   (B)　My dog is extremely friendly.
   (C)　We've been considering Spot.

3. Why do you dislike her?
   (A)　Because she is so friendly.
   (B)　Because I want to buy one.
   (C)　Because her attitude is negative.

4. Has he been invited to attend the affair at the president's home?
   (A)　Yes, in a democracy we vote for the president.
   (B)　Yes, his presence was requested by the president himself.
   (C)　No, the president will plan to have the party at his home.

5. Was the manager able to identify who took the money?
   (A) The money was found in his vehicle.
   (B) He found that an employee committed the crime.
   (C) They took his advice and borrowed a lot of money.

# Part 3　Short Conversation／会話問題

次の会話を聞いて、質問に最も適当な答えを選びなさい。

### 質問文パターン

* When 型パターン

1. **A**：The ring that I lost at the dance a week ago had belonged to my grandmother.
   **B**：No wonder you have been searching everywhere for it. Was it valuable?
   **A**：Yes, valuable to me. It reminded me of wonderful times at my grandmother's house when I was a child.

   **Q**：When was the ring lost?
   　　a. At the dance.　　　　b. Last week.
   　　c. When she was a child.　　d. It was valuable.

   解説：最初の文で話し手Aは「ダンスの時になくした」と述べている。

* How 型パターン

2. **A**：The police have offered a reward to anyone who helps them find the person who robbed the bank and hurt several witnesses.
   **B**：It's sad that someone tries to solve their financial problems with crime.
   **A**：I agree, but I'm hoping to solve my financial problems with that reward.

   **Q**：How are the police seeking help in finding the person who robbed the bank?
   　　a. Offering a reward.　　　　b. Hoping to solve financial problems.
   　　c. Hurting several witnesses.　　d. Solving the crime.

   解説：offer a reward「報酬を与える」。

* What 型パターン

3. **A**：One of the most important responsibilities of a citizen is voting. By voting a person has a voice in the government.
   **B**：In a democracy every person's vote counts the same as another person's vote.
   **A**：And every vote counts. In the last city election, the new mayor won by only 33 votes.

   **Q**：What does voting allow a citizen to do?
   　　a. The mayor was elected by only 33 votes.　　b. Lets every vote count.
   　　c. Have a voice in the government.　　　　　d. It's an important responsibility.

   解説：vote「投票する」、election「選挙」。count は「数える」の他に「重要である」という意味でも使われる。

\* Why 型パターン

4. **A**：I'm looking forward to seeing your family again.
   **B**：Well, Nick, they enjoyed meeting you when we visited in January and asked that I invite you again.
   **A**：So let's go. I'm ready.

   **Q**：Why has Nick been invited to visit the family?
   - a. Because they enjoyed his previous visit.
   - b. Because they have never met him before.
   - c. Because it's January and time for a visit.
   - d. Because they are looking forward to a trip.

解説：話し手Bが述べていることから、正解がAだとわかる。

# Part 4 Short Talks／説明文問題

次の説明文の質問に最も適当な答えを選びなさい。

### アメリカ人のダイエット

Over 60% of Americans have been on a diet at one time in their life, especially women. There have been thousands of different diets that people have tried throughout history, many of which are crazy and unhealthy ways to lose weight. One diet that was popular in the 1980s, for example, was the carrot diet. Women would eat only carrots for weeks at a time. The people on this diet would find that after a few days, their skin would turn orange like a carrot! The people on these all-fruit or all-vegetable diets also had no energy and felt tired all of the time. In the 1990s, companies came out with many different "low-fat" products. There were low-fat cheese, crackers, bread, frozen meals, ice cream, and anything you can think of. The problem with this is not only do people need some fat in their diets but these foods often had a great deal of sugar and unnatural ingredients. Finally, the recent low-carbohydrate diet has seen people eating less bread and potatoes, while eating primarily meat, eggs and vegetables. This, too, is unhealthy. What people need to do is eat small portions of a well-balanced diet and exercise if they want to lose weight.

1. What was one side-effect of people on the carrot diet?
    a. They wouldn't be able to sleep.　　b. They would have a lot of energy.
    c. Their skin would turn orange.　　d. They couldn't stop eating carrots.

2. What foods do people eliminate on a low-carbohydrate diet?
    a. Eggs.　　b. Vegetables.
    c. Bread and potatoes.　　d. Meat and fish.

解説：設問1　Carrot Diet をしている人たちは、何日か後に肌がオレンジ色になり、no energy 力がまったく無く、feel tired all the time「常に疲労感を感じていた」。正解－（C）

設問2　low-carbohydrate diet という名前のとおり、carbohydrate「炭水化物」の割合が low「低い」のだから、選択肢の炭水化物を選べばよい。正解－（C）

### 恐怖症

Are you so afraid of spiders that you run out of the house when you see one? Does the idea of speaking in front of other people make your hands start to shake and you start to sweat? Thousands of people around the world suffer from *phobias*, which are extreme fears of certain things that really can't hurt them. People who don't have phobias don't really understand the people who do. There are thousands of different kinds of phobias. Perhaps the most common phobia is the fear of speaking in public. Almost 70% of the people in one study said that they are afraid of it. Other common phobias include a fear of dogs, spiders, water, high places and flying. Some sound very strange to people but are not at all funny to the people who suffer from them. For example, one woman visited a doctor to get help for her fear of balloons. Another woman was afraid of mustard. If you are so afraid of something that it is affecting your life, see a doctor. There is help for phobias.

1. What is the most common kind of phobia?
	a. Fear of public speaking.　　b. Fear flying.
	c. Fear of mustard.　　d. Fear of balloons.

2. What percentage of the population suffers from the most common phobia?
	a. 49%.　　b. 55%.
	c. 60%.　　d. 70%.

**解説**：設問1　「most common phobia」最もよくある恐怖症は fear of speaking in public、つまり public speaking への恐怖である。正解－(A)

設問2　ある調査によると、70%の人が public speaking を恐れているのである。正解－(D)

## Part 5  Reading ／読解演習

次の段落文を読み、各設問に対して最も適切な答えを選びなさい（各段落速読問題は2分以内に終わらせなさい）。

### スピードリーディング

　Rodney was a successful writer from a very young age. When he was just in his early twenties, he was the head writer for *Late Night with David Letterman*, a very popular television show. Becoming the head writer for such a popular show is something many writers aspire to and never achieve. Rodney was living his dream at an age when many of his peers were still living at home.

　1. Which word best describes Rodney's occupation at the start of the article?
　　　a. Screenwriter.　　b. Comedian.
　　　c. Programmer.　　d. Novelist.

　2. According to the article, Rodney's first job was one that many people _____ .
　　　a. would not want.　　b. hope to get.
　　　c. could do with ease　　d. would find fault with

　The job was very demanding. Rodney usually worked sixty-hour weeks and had to come up with new jokes day after day. It is understandable how he became exhausted by the work. Eventually, Rodney quit his job as head writer and went to work as a freelance writer. A freelance writer does not work for any specific company but tries to sell his or her writing one piece at a time to whomever wants to buy it.

　1. How does the author describe Rodney's job?
　　　a. It paid Rodney very well.　　b. It made Rodney many friends.
　　　c. It kept Rodney from visiting his family.　　d. It required a lot from Rodney.

　2. Which word best describes a typical freelance writer, according to the definition given in the article?
　　　a. Unemployed.　　b. Self-employed.
　　　c. Lazy.　　d. Busy.

　Rodney did not have great success as a freelance writer. He lacked the discipline to be productive without someone making a lot of demands on his time, and so he mostly just did not do anything. At the time that Rodney was basically unemployed, many of his peers were working for Internet companies. At the time, everyone was very excited about the Internet—too excited, really. Bad decisions were being made. Management was not keeping the staff in line. Companies were spending money but not making any.

　1. During the time Rodney was a freelance writer, what sort of jobs were people he knew taking?
　　　a. Technology.　　b. Writing.
　　　c. Teaching.　　d. Finance.

2. Which of the following is a reason the article gives for Internet companies failing?
    a. Terrorism.        b. Poor management.
    c. High interest rates.    d. Bad stock market.

スピードリーディングで読んだものと同じ文を読みます。各設問に対して最も適切な答えを選びなさい。

**読解問題**

  Rodney was a successful writer from a very young age. When he was just in his early twenties, he was the head writer for *Late Night with David Letterman*, a very popular television show. Becoming the head writer for such a popular show is something many writers aspire to and never achieve. Rodney was living his dream at an age when many of his peers were still living at home.

  The job was very demanding. Rodney usually worked sixty-hour weeks and had to come up with new jokes day after day. It is understandable how he became exhausted by the work. Eventually, Rodney quit his job as head writer and went to work as a freelance writer. A freelance writer does not work for any specific company but tries to sell his or her writing one piece at a time to whomever wants to buy it.

  Rodney did not have great success as a freelance writer. He lacked the discipline to be productive without someone making a lot of demands on his time, and so he mostly just did not do anything. At the time that Rodney was basically unemployed, many of his peers were working for Internet companies. At the time, everyone was very excited about the Internet—too excited, really. Bad decisions were being made. Management was not keeping the staff in line. Companies were spending money but not making any.

  Rodney decided he might find something to write about by working at one of these companies. But instead of getting a job, he just showed up for work. Because so many employees were coming and going all the time, no one really noticed that Rodney did not belong. He wrote a very funny article about what it was like inside the company and became fairly famous for his documentation of what it was like on the Internet bubble just as it was bursting.

Comprehension Questions

1. Which of the following topics is this article concerned with?
    a. Education.      b. Finding a career.
    c. Big business.    d. The importance of family.

2. What best describes Rodney's reason for leaving his job?
    a. He was underpaid.    b. He missed home.
    c. He was overworked.    d. He wanted to help others.

3. What does the author say that Rodney needs to be productive?
    a. Supportive friends.    b. A demanding boss.
    c. A good wife.        d. Costly expenses.

4. For what did Rodney eventually become well-known?
    a. Writing a movie.    b. Returning to his job on television.
    c. Writing an article.    d. Entering politics.

# Part 6  Error Recognition／誤文訂正問題

各文には文法的な誤りがあります。訂正もしくは書き換えを必要とする語や語句を選びなさい。

1. It <u>looks</u> like a storm <u>is moving</u> in. We <u>should</u> <u>to shut</u> the windows.
   　　 A 　　　　　　　　　B 　　　　　 C 　　 D

   解説：should は助動詞 shall の過去形であり、続く動詞は必ず原形動詞でないといけない。本文には不定詞が来ているので、to をはずすことで文章が正される。

   正しい英文：It looks like a storm is moving in. We should shut the windows.

2. Summer vacation <u>begins</u> on May 13. We <u>do</u> <u>have to</u> go to classes again <u>until</u> August 29.
   　　　　　　　　　　 A 　　　　　　　　　B 　C 　　　　　　　　　　 D

   解説：2文目の do have to は have to の強調形で文法的に正しいが、内容的におかしい。よって「学校が8月までない」という意味にするため do の後に not を挿入する。

   正しい英文：Summer vacation begins on May 13. We don't have to go to classes again until August 29.

3. Excuse me, I <u>didn't</u> <u>heard</u> what you <u>said</u>. Could you <u>repeat</u> your last sentence?
   　　　　　　　 A 　　 B 　　　　　　 C 　　　　　　 D

   解説：最初の下線部2つに注目する。過去否定文を表す didn't があるのに続く動詞が過去形のままであり、文法的に間違っている。よって heard を hear に書き直す。

   正しい英文：Excuse me, I didn't hear what you said. Could you repeat your last sentence?

4. I <u>enjoyed</u> my teenage years <u>immensely</u>. When my girlfriends and I <u>get</u> together, we would <u>do</u> anything
   　 A 　　　　　　　　　　　 B 　　　　　　　　　　　　　　 C 　　　　　　　　　　 D
   and everything to have fun.

   解説：1文目で明らかに過去の話をしているので、2文目も時制を合わさないといけない。よって現在形の動詞 get を過去形の got に直す。

   正しい英文：I enjoyed my teenage years immensely. When my girlfriends and I got together, we would do anything and everything to have fun.

5. I <u>don't</u> enjoy <u>to play</u> sports. I would <u>much</u> rather <u>study</u> economics.
   　 A 　　　　　 B 　　　　　　　　 C 　　　　 D

   解説：enjoy は動名詞をとる動詞なので、本文にある不定詞は不適切な表現になる。よって to play は playing に正されるべき。

   正しい英文：I don't enjoy playing sports. I would much rather study economics.

6. In the <u>last</u> couple of years, I've <u>gone</u> to Mexico, Nepal, and India. I like <u>to take</u> <u>tripping</u>.
   　　　 A 　　　　　　　　　　 B 　　　　　　　　　　　　　　　　　　　　　 C 　　 D

   解説：take trips で「旅行する」という表現。よって現在分詞の tripping はおかしい。tripping を trips に直す必要がある。

   正しい英文：In the last couple of years, I've gone to Mexico, Nepal, and India. I like to take trips.

7. The recent tragedy in West Virginia resulted for the deaths of more than thirty young students.
         A                                B        C              D

   Answer: C (for → in)

   解説：resulted in で「〜と言う結果になる」という言い回しなので result for はおかしい。よって前置詞を
   for から in に書き換える。

   正しい英文：The recent tragedy in West Virginia resulted in the deaths of more than thirty young students.

## Part 7　Incomplete Sentence／文法・語彙問題

文法的に適切な語や語句を1つ選び、文を完成させなさい。

1. It really doesn't matter what she wears to school. Why don't you let her _____ up her own mind?
   - a. make
   - b. to make
   - c. made
   - d. makes

   訳：彼女が学校に何を着ていこうかなんてどうでもいいことです。自分で選ばせたらどうですか？
   解説：使役動詞 let＋人＋原形動詞で「人に〜させる」となる。よって下線部には原形動詞のAが当てはまる。

2. We just went to the doctor, and now we are going to the pharmacy to have our prescription _____.
   - a. filling
   - b. be full
   - c. filled
   - d. fulfill

   訳：医者に行ってきたので、これから薬局へ処方箋の薬を取りに行こうと思う。
   解説：文章がS＋V＋O＋Cの第5文型で締めくくられている事に注意する。下線部が目的語 our prescription の補語になるので、「詰められた」と言う意味になる過去文詞の形容詞用法がこの場合正しい答えになる。よって正解はC。

3. The movie stars wouldn't let the press _____ their pictures.
   - a. to take
   - b. took
   - c. taking
   - d. take

   訳：映画俳優は報道陣に写真をとらせたりはしません。
   解説：使役動詞 let＋人＋原形動詞で「人に〜させる」となる。よって下線部には原形動詞のDが当てはまる。

4. Looking at his motorcycle after the accident made him _____ that he was very lucky to be alive.
   - a. realize
   - b. to realize
   - c. realized
   - d. had realized

   訳：事故の後に壊れた自分のバイクを目にし、死なずにすんだのは本当に幸運なことであったと自覚した。
   解説：使役動詞 make＋人＋原形動詞で「人に〜させる」となる。よって下線部には原形動詞のAが当てはまる。

5. "Are those new condominiums?" "No, those are my _____ new offices."
   - a. bosses'
   - b. bosse's
   - c. boss's
   - d. boss is

   訳：「あれは新しい分譲マンションですか？」「いいえ、あれは私の上司達の事務所です」
   解説：boss で「上司」となるが、本文は複数形なので bosses になる。「上司達の」と所有格の's がつけたいのだが、語尾がすでに's' なのでこの場合はそのままアポストロフィーが付く形になる。よって正解はAになる。

# Lesson 12 （http://audio.lincenglish.com にアクセスして音声を聞いてください）

## Part 1　Image Listening／写真描写問題

1. 左の写真を見て、人物の行動や物の位置などについて文を3つ作りなさい。
   _____
   _____

2. 写真の描写文として最も適切な文をA～Dの中から選びなさい。
   （A），（B），（C），（D）

1. 左の写真を見て、人物の行動や物の位置などについて文を3つ作りなさい。
   _____
   _____

2. 写真の描写文として最も適切な文をA～Dの中から選びなさい。
   （A），（B），（C），（D）

1. 左の写真を見て、人物の行動や物の位置などについて文を3つ作りなさい。
   _____
   _____

2. 写真の描写文として最も適切な文をA～Dの中から選びなさい。
   （A），（B），（C），（D）

1. 左の写真を見て、人物の行動や物の位置などについて文を3つ作りなさい。
   _____
   _____

2. 写真の描写文として最も適切な文をA～Dの中から選びなさい。
   （A），（B），（C），（D）

# Part 2　Question and Response／質疑応答問題

## 重要な質問表現

Are those two men twins?
　　twins「双子」。三つ子は triplets、四つ子は quadruplets、五つ子は quintuplets と呼ばれる。

Can this portable DVD player work in all countries?
　　portable「携帯用の・持ち運びに便利な」。

Can you help me solve my problem?
　　solve「（問題などを）解決する」。

Why does he earn such good grades in every class he takes?
　　grade「成績の評価・評点」。米国の大学などの標準的な成績評価法では、A-excellent（秀）、B-good（優）、
　　C-fair（良）、D-minimum passing（可）、F-failed（不可）が使われている。

I was in the laboratory and found out by mistake.
　　by mistake「誤って・間違いにより」。

How did he promote his business when he first opened it?
　　business「商売・事業」。営利を目的とする意味合いが強い語。

What book are you packing for your journey to Europe?
　　pack「（物を箱などに）詰める・入れる」。

Was the psychologist able to help you overcome your fear of heights?
　　fear of heights「高所恐怖」。fear はある行為や事態に伴って起こるかもしれないことへの不安・懸念という
　　意味で用いられる。

Does the punishment fit the crime?
　　fit「（物事が）条件にかなった・適した・ふさわしい」。

Would you mind if I participate in this discussion?
　　participate「（事に）参加・関与する」。主に行動面での積極的な参加の意。

## 確認ドリル

次の1～5の質問に対して最も適切な応答をそれぞれ（A）～（C）の中から選びなさい。

1. When composing a photo, where should you place the person or thing of interest?
   (A) The philosopher questions the value of photos.
   (B) Anywhere except in the center of the photo.
   (C) Photography is a hobby enjoyed by many people.

2. Did you notice how nervous he was when he presented his speech?
   (A) It was such an interesting speech.
   (B) I saw that his hands were shaking.
   (C) After the speech, he told me he was fairly satisfied.

3. When did you first suspect that he had committed the crime?
   (A) I was able to identify him to the police.
   (B) After I learned about his background.
   (C) Violent crime is especially frightening.

4. Which drug did the doctor recommend?
   (A) I took the drug twice yesterday.
   (B) One for treatment of pain.
   (C) The pill is tiny.

5. Are the citizens in that country governed by a good leader?
   (A) Yes, the landscape of that country is beautiful.
   (B) No, he's terrible. The citizens are planning a revolution.
   (C) No, he is a politician, not a soldier.

# Part 3　Short Conversation／会話問題

次の会話を聞いて、質問に最も適当な答えを選びなさい。

## 質問文パターン

### ＊ How 型パターン

1. **A**：Let's go to a furniture store to look for a shelving unit that can hold our television, music system, and DVD's.
   **B**：We'll need to measure the height, width, and depth of our equipment.
   **A**：Good idea. We also need to know the size of the space where we want to put the shelves. I'll get a measuring tzape.

   **Q**：How will they determine the height, width, and depth of the shelving unit they need?
   　　a. Measure the equipment and the space.　　b. Go to a furniture store.
   　　c. Buy a television, music system, and DVD's.　　d. Ask the clerk at the furniture store.

   解説：measure「測る」。

### ＊ When 型パターン

2. **A**：Our military unit encountered the enemy at sunset. After a brief exchange of gunfire, the enemy disappeared. As soon as possible, we returned to our camp.
   **B**：Has your unit received its commands for tomorrow?
   **A**：We're to return to the same location and occupy the town.

   **Q**：When did the soldiers fight the enemy?
   　　a. Tomorrow.　　b. At sunset.
   　　c. At the same location.　　d. As soon as possible.

   解説：encounter「遭遇する」。

### ＊ What 型パターン

3. **A**：I like that coffee shop. The current manager has transformed it. The employees are efficient and the drinks are good.
   **B**：You certainly sound impressed. Let's stop there on our way home.
   **A**：O.K. I hope you won't be disappointed.

   **Q**：What caused the improvements in the coffee shop to occur?
   　　a. The reputation of the manager.　　b. Efficient employees have been hired.
   　　c. Good coffee is served.　　d. Changes made by the manager.

   解説：最初の話し手Ａの文から正解はＤとわかる。

\* Where 型パターン

4. **A**：Have you run that test yet?
   **B**：Yes, the chemicals have been identified.
   **A**：Be sure to include all of the information in your report.

   **Q**：Where is this conversation taking place?
   　　　a. Newspaper office.　　　b. Desert.
   　　　c. Urban neighborhood.　　d. Laboratory.

解説：run a test は「テストをする」という意味。

# Part 4  Short Talks ／説明文問題

次の説明文の質問に最も適当な答えを選びなさい。

### 長寿国の日本

Throughout the world, different countries have different life expectancies. Life expectancy is the age to which the average person is expected to live. Many factors can contribute to different life expectancies, including economy, health care, and lifestyle. Researchers are finding that a person's lifestyle has a huge influence on life expectancy. Lifestyle refers to what you eat, how much exercise you get, how much stress is in your life, and if you have any unhealthy habits such as smoking or drinking too much alcohol. The country in the world with the highest life expectancy is Japan, at an average age of 80 years. The U.S., however, is ranked 24th in the world, with a life expectancy of 71 years old. Since more than 60% of Americans are overweight, scientists believe this is largely due to eating too many unhealthy foods and not getting enough exercise. In Japan, people eat a lot of vegetables, fish and rice, whereas in the U.S. people eat a lot of fast food and snacks like potato chips. In Japan, more people lead active lifestyles, whereas in the U.S., many people are couch potatoes. Americans can learn a lot from the Japanese lifestyle.

1. What is the average life expectancy in Japan?
   a. 100 years old.      b. 71 years old.
   c. 80 years old.       d. 99 years old.

2. What percentage of Americans is overweight?
   a. 20%.     b. 40%.
   c. 60%.     d. 25%.

解説： 設問 1　日本の平均寿命は世界一とされ、an average age of 80 years「平均寿命 80 歳」となっている。正解－（C）

　　　設問 2　overweight は obese と同じ肥満という意味で over 60% of Americans「アメリカ国民の 60% 以上」が肥満を抱えている。正解－（C）

### ドリフト・ドライビング

Drift driving is a pastime that is becoming more and more popular in different countries around the world. When people drift, they cause their car to move sideways instead of forward. One way to do this is to use the emergency brake. Another way is to shift down into lower gears while traveling at high speeds. Drift driving takes two different forms. On the one hand, it is a controlled sport that is done with protective clothing on a closed racetrack. The other form is driving illegally in regular traffic, putting the lives of others at risk. Such activities take place in many locations, such as Japan, Hawaii and Saudi Arabia. A recent video on the Internet shows young men in Saudi Arabia dangerously drift driving through busy traffic on a regular highway. Other times, they do it a little more safely on the sand away from traffic. There have been several deaths involved in illegal drift driving. One time, the driver ran into the crowd, killing several people. In Japan, one famous drift driver is eiichi Tsuchiya, also known as the Drift King.

1. What are two ways to cause a car to drift?
   - a. Hitting a patch of ice.
   - b. Using the emergency brake and lower gears.
   - c. Turning off the car while driving at high speeds.
   - d. Buying a car specially made for drifting.

2. Although it is always dangerous, what is the safest way to drift drive?
   - a. In busy, regular highway traffic.
   - b. On curves in the mountains.
   - c. On neighborhood streets.
   - d. On a contained racetrack with a helmet.

解説：設問1　車をdrift「横滑り」させる方法とは、前進中にemergency brake「サイドブレーキ」を使うことと、速い速度で前進中にギアを低いものに切り替えることである。正解－(B)

設問2　ドリフト運転の2つの方法とは、racetrack「レース場」でprotective clothing「体を保護する衣服」を装着して行われるやり方と、行動でillegal「違法的」に行われる方法がある。正解－(D)

# Part 5  Reading／読解演習

次の段落文を読み、各設問に対して最も適切な答えを選びなさい（各段落速読問題は2分以内に終わらせなさい）。

### スピードリーディング

Tom is a teacher of law and philosophy. Although Tom never went to law school, many of his students are lawyers. The rest of his students are philosophers. Tom has the expertise to teach about the law because he spent many years studying how the law is supposed to work and how the law actually works. In fact, after more than forty years of teaching about the law, Tom knows more about it than most lawyers.

1. How much does Tom know about the law?
   a. As much as anyone else.      b. As much as a good philosophy student.
   c. As much as a few lawyers.    d. As much as an expert.

2. How long has Tom been teaching about the law?
   a. Four years.       b. Four decades.
   c. Four semesters.   d. Four centuries.

Tom is interested specifically in critical legal studies. The idea behind this field is that there is an ideal notion of how the law is supposed to work. It is embodied in the statue of justice that you may have seen: a blindfolded woman holding a set of scales. Justice is intended to fairly balance the interests of any two people subjected to the law without respect to who those people are, or how much money or power they possess, or anything else that would be unfair to consider in determining right and wrong.

1. The statue of justice is a _____ representation of an idea.
   a. Literal.    b. Digital.
   c. Visual.     d. Metaphorical.

2. Which principle does the article imply is most important to justice?
   a. Dignity.    b. Scales.
   c. Love        d. Equality.

The field of critical legal studies looks for ways in which the law is written so that equal justice is not the result. Sometimes, these are relatively straightforward, as when some parts of the United States had laws that explicitly treated black people to a different set of rules than white people. Thankfully, these laws no longer exist. But there are still ways, for instance, in which laws favor people who have wealth over those who do not. This is what Tom studies.

1. Straightforward instances of injustice are _____.
   a. plain to see.      b. difficult to notice.
   c. subtle            d. dangerous

2. Which group does the article say that United States law sometimes favors unjustly?
   a. Athletic.   b. Rich.
   c. Smart.     d. Handsome.

スピードリーディングで読んだものと同じ文を読みます。各設問に対して最も適切な答えを選びなさい。

### 読解問題

Tom is a teacher of law and philosophy. Although Tom never went to law school, many of his students are lawyers. The rest of his students are philosophers. Tom has the expertise to teach about the law because he spent many years studying how the law is supposed to work and how the law actually works. In fact, after more than forty years of teaching about the law, Tom knows more about it than most lawyers.

Tom is interested specifically in critical legal studies. The idea behind this field is that there is an ideal notion of how the law is supposed to work. It is embodied in the statue of justice that you may have seen: a blindfolded woman holding a set of scales. Justice is intended to fairly balance the interests of any two people subjected to the law without respect to who those people are, or how much money or power they possess, or anything else that would be unfair to consider in determining right and wrong.

The field of critical legal studies looks for ways in which the law is written so that equal justice is not the result. Sometimes, these are relatively straightforward, as when some parts of the United States had laws that explicitly treated black people to a different set of rules than white people. Thankfully, these laws no longer exist. But there are still ways, for instance, in which laws favor people who have wealth over those who do not. This is what Tom studies.

It is also what Tom teaches future lawyers to be aware of. Law school is a lot like a trade school, a place that would train someone to be a plumber or an electrician. Law school teaches what the law is and how to use it; it does not encourage lawyers to think about why laws are written the way they are or who might benefit because of it. Tom teaches lawyers a philosophical perspective on their occupation. In doing so, he hopes to create both better lawyers and better laws.

Comprehension Questions

1. Who makes up the majority of Tom's students?
   a. Lawyers.
   b. Oother teachers.
   c. Students who haven't decided what they want to do.
   d. Philosophers.

2. On what does Tom's study of the law focus?
   a. How much money is needed to represent a client.
   b. Whether a client is guilty or innocent.
   c. How to win cases.
   d. The difference between the ideal and ctual conditions of justice.

3. Ideally, how should the chances for someone with a lot of power compare to the chances of someone with very little power if they face each other in court?

a. Their chances of succeeding should be equal.
b. The powerful should have an advantage over the less powerful.
c. The less powerful should have an advantage over the powerful.
d. It will depend from case to case.

4. Which of the following does Tom hope will result from training better lawyers?
   a. Better teachers.
   b. Better students.
   c. Better laws.
   d. Better judges.

## Part 6　Error Recognition／誤文訂正問題

各文には文法的な誤りがあります。訂正もしくは書き換えを必要とする語や語句を選びなさい。

1. Yesterday afternoon we attended a bicycle <u>fair</u> and found a <u>tremendous</u> number of <u>mechanical</u> pieces for
　　　　　　　　　　　　　　　　　　　　　A　　　　　　　　　B　　　　　　　　　　　C

   <u>used</u> in building free bicycles.
   D

   解説：for use in で「〜に利用できる」という表現。よって4つ目の下線部の過去分詞 used は名詞の use に直す。

   正しい英文：Yesterday afternoon we attended a bicycle fair and found a tremendous number of mechanical pieces for use in building free bicycles.

2. The <u>crew</u> is <u>composed</u> of <u>volunteers</u>; I am hopeful that there are experienced <u>construct</u> workers among them.
   　　A　　　　B　　　　　C　　　　　　　　　　　　　　　　　　　　　　　　　D

   解説：construction workers で「土木作業員」と言う意味で、文中の construct workers は不自然。よって construct を construction に訂正する。

   正しい英文：The crew is composed of volunteers; I am hopeful that there are experienced construction workers among them.

3. I was <u>discouraged</u> to learn how <u>expensive</u> the tickets were. I may not be able to visit the <u>ruined</u>.
   　　　　A　　　　　　　　　　　　B　　　　　　　　　　　　　　　　　　　　　　　　C

   解説：最後の下線部が動詞 visit の目的語であるべきなのに、形容詞になっている。よって ruined を名詞の ruins に直す。

   正しい英文：I was discouraged to learn how expensive the tickets were. I may not be able to visit the ruins.

4. I was truly <u>amazing</u> <u>to learn</u> that the auction had brought in sixty <u>grand</u> for the museum's building <u>fund</u>.
   　　　　　　A　　　　　B　　　　　　　　　　　　　　　　　　C　　　　　　　　　　　　　　　D

   解説：I was amazing という表現は「私は驚くほどにすごい」となり、内容がおかしくなる。よって1つ目の下線の現在分詞は過去分詞に直し、受動態にしなければならない。

   正しい英文：I was truly amazed to learn that the auction had brought in sixty grand for the museum's building fund.

5. I might have <u>misunderstand</u>; however, I do not <u>think</u> a person can be brought to <u>trial</u> without an indictment
   　　　　　　　A　　　　　　　　　　　　　　B　　　　　　　　　　　　C

   by the <u>grand</u> jury.
   　　　　D

   解説：might have ＋過去分詞で「〜であったかもしれない」という表現である。よって完了形を表す have の後の動詞は原型の misunderstand ではなく、過去分詞形の misunderstood でないといけない。

   正しい英文：I might have misunderstood; however, I do not think a person can be brought to trial without an indictment by the grand jury.

6. I am <u>embarrassed</u> <u>to admit</u> that I fell into such an obvious <u>trapped</u>. I will not be so easy to <u>trick</u> next time.
　　　　　　　A　　　　B　　　　　　　　　　　　　　　C　　　　　　　　　　　　　　D

　　解説：such a 形容詞＋名詞で「そんな（形容詞）な（名詞）」という表現。よって3つ目の下線の過去分詞は間違いである。名詞の trap がこの場合正しい答え。

　　正しい英文：I am embarrassed to admit that I fell into such an obvious trap. I will not be so easy to trick next time.

7. Mona told me that she has been <u>diagnose</u> with <u>lung</u> cancer. The news was <u>difficult</u> <u>to hear</u>.
　　　　　　　　　　　　　　　　　　A　　　　　　B　　　　　　　　　　　　C　　　D

　　解説：has been で完了形の受動態を表しているので、それに続く動詞はもちろん受動態の形で過去分詞形でないといけない。よって diagnose を diagnosed に書き直すと文章が成り立つ。

　　正しい英文：Mona told me that she has been diagnosed with lung cancer. The news was difficult to hear.

# Part 7　Incomplete Sentence ／文法・語彙問題

文法的に適切な語や語句を 1 つ選び、文を完成させなさい。

1. The jewelry advertisement appeals to young, engaged couples by declaring that the rings will _____ as long as their love.
    - a. endure
    - b. endured
    - c. enduring
    - d. to endure

   訳：「指輪は愛情とを同じだけ長持ちする」という売り文句の広告が若いカップルの注目を集めている。
   解説：will は助動詞なので続く下線部は単純に原形動詞でないといけない理由から A を選ぶのが正しい。

2. I do not believe the library has set any _____ on the number of books you can check out; however, there are limits on CDs and other audio material.
    - a. limitedation
    - b. limitations
    - c. limiting
    - d. to limit

   訳：図書館で貸出冊数に制限はないはずですが、CD などの音響機材には制限があります。
   解説：any は複数形名詞を修飾する形容詞なので、続く名詞は B しかあてはまらない。

3. I am not _____ to driving at night and so was grateful to arrive home safely last evening after coming through heavy traffic and a rainstorm.
    - a. to accustom
    - b. accustomed
    - c. accustoms
    - d. to accustomed

   訳：夜道を運転し慣れていないのに、昨晩無事に交通渋滞と大雨を繰りぬけて帰宅できたことをうれしく思った。
   解説：be accustomed to ＋名詞で「～に慣れている」という熟語。本文はこの表現の否定文となる。選択肢からは B の accustomed を選ぶ。

4. On the mountain above our town, we can see the _____ lines of a lake that covered our valley some 15,000 to 12,000 years ago, toward the end of the last Ice Age.
    - a. shores
    - b. shored
    - c. shore
    - d. shoring

   訳：街の北にある山では、私たちは 15,000 ～ 12,000 年前から氷河期末期にかけて渓谷を埋め尽くしたとされる湖の海岸線を目にすることができます。
   解説：shore lines で「海岸線」という表現なので、C の shore が正解となる。

5. Retrieving a stick is not so much a _____ for a dog, but rather a trait of the dog's breed.
    - a. trick
    - b. tricked
    - c. tricks
    - d. tricky

   訳：犬にとって、棒を拾ってくるのは技ではなく、むしろある特定の犬種に備わった本能であるといえよう。
   解説：冠詞に続き、下線後に名詞がないので、下線自体が名詞であり、単数形でないといけない。よって A の trick が最も正しい答えとなる。

# 解答

## Lesson 1

**Part 1　Image Listening:**
1. B
2. C
3. A
4. B

**Part 2　Question and Response:**
Drills:
1. C
2. C
3. C
4. A
5. C

**Part 3　Short Conversation:**
1. B
2. C
3. B
4. C

**Part 4　Short Talks:**
First paragraph
1. C
2. D
Second paragraph:
1. C
2. A

**Part 5　Speed Reading:**
First paragraph:
1. A
2. D
Second paragraph:
1. C
2. B
Third paragraph:
1. C
2. B
Comprehension Questions:
1. B
2. C
3. B
4. C

**Part 6　Error Recognition:**
1. C
2. C
3. A
4. C
5. B
6. D
7. B

**Part 7　Incomplete Sentence:**
1. B
2. D
3. C
4. C
5. D

## Lesson 2

**Part 1　Image Listening:**
1. A
2. B
3. C
4. B

**Part 2　Question and Response:**
Drills:
1. A
2. A
3. B
4. A
5. B

**Part 3　Short Conversation:**
1. B
2. C
3. C
4. C

**Part 4　Short Talks:**
First paragraph
1. C
2. D
Second paragraph:
1. B
2. D

**Part 5　Speed Reading:**
First paragraph:
1. A
2. D
Second paragraph:
1. C
2. C
Third paragraph:
1. B
2. B
Comprehension Questions:
1. B
2. C
3. C
4. C

**Part 6　Error Recognition:**
1. B
2. D
3. C
4. C
5. D
6. C
7. D

**Part 7　Incomplete Sentence:**
1. C
2. D
3. D
4. B
5. C

## Lesson 3

Part 1　Image Listening:
1. D
2. A
3. A
4. C

Part 2　Question and Response:
Drills:
1. B
2. B
3. B
4. B
5. A

Part 3　Short Conversation:
1. D
2. C
3. D
4. A

Part 4　Short Talks:
First paragraph
1. C
2. A
Second paragraph:
1. D
2. A

Part 5　Speed Reading:
First paragraph:
1. A
2. D
Second paragraph:
1. D
2. C
Third paragraph:
1. C
2. A
Comprehension Questions:
1. B
2. C

3. B
4. C

Part 6　Error Recognition:
1. C
2. D
3. A
4. C
5. D
6. D
7. B

Part 7　Incomplete Sentence:
1. D
2. C
3. B
4. C
5. D

## Lesson 4

Part 1　Image Listening:
1. A
2. C
3. C
4. B

Part 2　Question and Response:
Drills:
1. C
2. C
3. B
4. B
5. C

Part 3　Short Conversation:
1. C
2. A
3. B
4. C

Part 4　Short Conversation:
First paragraph
1. C
2. B
Second paragraph:
1. A
2. D

Part 5　Speed Reading:
First paragraph:
1. A
2. D
Second paragraph:
1. C
2. B
Third paragraph:
1. A
2. B
Comprehension Questions:
1. B
2. C
3. C
4. C

Part 6　Error Recognition:
1. A
2. D
3. A
4. A
5. B
6. B
7. D

Part 7　Incomplete Sentence:
1. B
2. C
3. A
4. C
5. B

## Lesson 5

Part 1  Image Listening:
1. C
2. B
3. C
4. D

Part 2  Question and Response:
Drills:
1. A
2. B
3. C
4. A
5. C

Part 3  Short Conversation:
1. B
2. A
3. A
4. A

Part 4  Short Talks:
First paragraph
1. B
2. B
Second paragraph:
1. A
2. D

Part 5  Speed Reading:
First paragraph:
1. B
2. D
Second paragraph:
1. D
2. C
Third paragraph:
1. B
2. B
Comprehension Questions:
1. D
2. C

3. C
4. D

Part 6  Error Recognition:
1. A
2. B
3. C
4. C
5. B
6. C
7. C

Part 7  Incomplete Sentence:
1. D
2. C
3. B
4. D
5. B

## Lesson 6

Part 1  Image Listening:
1. B
2. B
3. A
4. D

Part 2  Question and Response:
Drills:
1. A
2. C
3. B
4. A
5. A

Part 3  Short Conversation:
1. B
2. A
3. B
4. B

Part 4  Short Talks:
First paragraph
1. D
2. D
Second paragraph:
1. D
2. C

Part 5  Speed Reading:
First paragraph:
1. C
2. B
Second paragraph:
1. D
2. A
Third paragraph:
1. B
2. D
Comprehension Questions:
1. B
2. C
3. C
4. A

Part 6  Error Recognition:
1. A
2. C
3. C
4. B
5. A
6. C
7. D

Part 7  Incomplete Sentence:
1. A
2. D
3. D
4. B
5. A

# Lesson 7

Part 1　Image Listening:
1. A
2. C
3. B
4. A

Part 2　Question and Response:
Drills:
1. C
2. C
3. A
4. B
5. A

Part 3　Short Conversation:
1. C
2. D
3. B
4. A

Part 4　Short Talks:
First paragraph
1. A
2. C
Second paragraph:
1. B
2. D

Part 5　Speed Reading:
First paragraph:
1. B
2. D
Second paragraph:
1. A
2. B
Third paragraph:
1. C
2. B
Comprehension Questions:
1. B
2. D

3. C
4. B

Part 6　Error Recognition:
1. B
2. C
3. D
4. D
5. B
6. A
7. A

Part 7　Incomplete Sentence:
1. B
2. C
3. B
4. B
5. B

# Lesson 8

Part 1　Image Listening:
1. D
2. A
3. A
4. C

Part 2　Question and Response:
Drills:
1. A
2. B
3. B
4. C
5. B

Part 3　Short Conversation:
1. A
2. A
3. B
4. C

Part 4　Short Talks:
First paragraph
1. B
2. C
Second paragraph:
1. D
2. A

Part 5　Speed Reading:
First paragraph:
1. C
2. D
Second paragraph:
1. B
2. C
Third paragraph:
1. A
2. B
Comprehension Questions:
1. B
2. C
3. B
4. A

Part 6　Error Recognition:
1. C
2. B
3. A
4. A
5. B
6. C
7. B

Part 7　Incomplete Sentence:
1. A
2. C
3. C
4. D
5. C

**Lesson 9**

Part 1   Image Listening:
1. D
2. B
3. A
4. D

Part 2   Question and Response:
Drills:
1. B
2. A
3. B
4. B
5. A

Part 3   Short Conversation:
1. C
2. D
3. D
4. D

Part 4   Short Talks:
First paragraph
1. D
2. D
Second paragraph:
1. C
2. A

Part 5   Speed Reading:
First paragraph:
1. B
2. C
Second paragraph:
1. C
2. B
Third paragraph:
1. C
2. A
Comprehension Questions:
1. B
2. C

3. B
4. C

Part 6   Error Recognition:
1. A
2. B
3. A
4. B
5. D
6. D
7. A

Part 7   Incomplete Sentence:
1. B
2. D
3. B
4. A
5. A

**Lesson 10**

Part 1   Image Listening:
1. C
2. A
3. D
4. C

Part 2   Question and Response:
Drills:
1. B
2. C
3. C
4. B
5. C

Part 3   Short Conversation:
1. B
2. B
3. C
4. C

Part 4   Short Talks:
First paragraph
1. A
2. B
Second paragraph:
1. B
2. B

Part 5   Speed Reading:
First paragraph:
1. A
2. B
Second paragraph:
1. D
2. C
Third paragraph:
1. C
2. B
Comprehension Questions:
1. A
2. B
3. C
4. D

Part 6   Error Recognition:
1. C
2. D
3. C
4. D
5. A
6. B
7. C

Part 7   Incomplete Sentence:
1. C
2. B
3. C
4. B
5. A

**Lesson 11**

Part 1　Image Listening:
1. D
2. C
3. A
4. B

Part 2　Question and Response:
Drills:
1. A
2. C
3. C
4. B
5. B

Part 3　Short Conversation:
1. B
2. A
3. C
4. A

Part 4　Short Talks:
First paragraph
1. C
2. C
Second paragraph:
1. A
2. D

Part 5　Speed Reading:
First paragraph:
1. A
2. B
Second paragraph:
1. D
2. B
Third paragraph:
1. A
2. B
Comprehension Questions:
1. B
2. C
3. B
4. C

Part 6　Error Recognition:
1. D
2. B
3. B
4. C
5. B
6. D
7. C

Part 7　Incomplete Sentence:
1. A
2. C
3. D
4. A
5. C

**Lesson 12**

Part 1　Image Listening:
1. D
2. C
3. D
4. B

Part 2　Question and Response:
Drills:
1. B
2. B
3. B
4. B
5. B

Part 3　Short Conversation:
1. A
2. B
3. D
4. D

Part 4　Short Talks:
First paragraph
1. C
2. C
Second paragraph:
1. B
2. D

Part 5　Speed Reading:
First paragraph:
1. D
2. B
Second paragraph:
1. C
2. D
Third paragraph:
1. A
2. B
Comprehension Questions:
1. A
2. D
3. A
4. C

Part 6　Error Recognition:
1. D
2. B
3. D
4. A
5. A
6. C
7. A

Part 7　Incomplete Sentence:
1. A
2. B
3. B
4. C
5. A

## ■編者紹介

Linc Educational Resources, Inc

　米国大学の英語教育専門家の協力を得ながら、総合メディアによる実用的な英語学習教材の製作に携わっているカリキュラム開発組織。また、短期留学企画・制作、正規留学支援プログラムの運営、アメリカの大学への編入および単位移行もサポートしている。実践的な英語運用能力の開発を支援するための情報収集、オンライン教材開発を主たる活動内容としている。Linc English、Linc Kids（児童、児童英語教育者対象）の執筆・編集を行うとともに、e-ラーニングのシステムの構築、オンライン上での学習管理も行っている。

## ■監修者・編著者紹介

橘　由加　（たちばな　ゆか）

仙台市出身

東北大学高等教育開発推進センター准教授。

モンタナ大学近代・古典言語文学部准教授（兼任）。

カリフォルニア大学　国際関係学修士課程修了。

東北大学　言語情報学博士課程修了。

　モンタナ大学で日本語学、日米比較文化論、日本文化の准教授として勤務。また、大学内にあるマンスフィールドセンター（国際会議）の通訳も兼ねる。

　2008年度から東北大学高等教育推進開発センターに所属。全学の英語教育改革推進アドバイザーも兼ね、教授陣たちに CALL 教授法を指導。

LINC 教材開発顧問。「Linc English オンライン・カリキュラムコース」の開発、監修・編著に携わる。

著　書

『アメリカの大学教育の現状』三修社、『大学外国語教育改革』熊本大学文学部文学科（共著）、他。

## ■ Linc English について

　モンタナ大学准教授の橘由加氏を中心に、米国の大学の外国語教育の専門家によって開発された。コンテンツ制作者・文法解説・翻訳者は全員米国の大学で ESL/TESOL のトレーニングを受け、言語学、英語学の修士号の資格を持っている。モンタナ大学のコンピュータ・サイエンス、言語学の専門家を中心にチームを編成し、ワシントン大学、カリフォルニア州立大学（ロングビーチ校）、サンフランシスコ州立大学から日米の ESL/TESOL の専門家を集め、米国のカリキュラム開発会社 Linc による出資にて、216レッスン、A4判で18,000ページ以上にのぼる莫大なオンライン・コンテンツを、4年を費やし開発した。Linc English は音声をとおしてリスニング、読解、文法・語彙力の向上を目指す。また学習・成績管理が容易にでき、英語力がどのように向上しているか管理できるプログラムになっている。忙しい英語教員にとって、学習者の成績管理が容易にでき、採点もしてくれる、という学習管理システムがあるのは非常にありがたいものだろう。Linc English はオンライン上で非常に簡単に使え、ユーザーフレンドリーなので、テクノロジーに強くない学習者、教員でも使いこなせることが魅力でもある。費用も経済的な価格で設定されている。個人で購入した場合の1年間の全コースは216レッスンでアクセス費用は39,600円。団体購入の場合、1人当たりの1年間のアクセス費用は受講者数によっても異なるが、6,000円から10,000円前後となる。

[商品に関するお問い合わせ]

Linc Educational Resources, Inc.

　666-0145　兵庫県川西市けやき坂 1-18-113

　ディレクター　笈田美佐

　Tel：072-799-3566/mobile：090-7878-5776

　URL：www.lincenglish.com　www.lincamerica.com

　e-メール：linc_english@jttk.zaq.ne.jp

[商品・本書に関するお問い合わせ]

（株）大学教育出版

　700-0953　岡山市西市 855-4

　URL：www.kyoiku.co.jp

　E メール：info@kyouiku.co.jp

オンライン英語学習用テキスト
## Linc English　GOLD I
2008 年 10 月 10 日　初版第 1 刷発行

■監修者・編著者────橘　由加
■編　　　　　者────Linc Educational Resources, Inc
■発　行　者────佐藤　守
■発　行　所────株式会社 大学教育出版
　　　　　　　　〒 700-0953　岡山市西市 855-4
　　　　　　　　電話（086）244-1268　FAX（086）246-0294
■印　刷　製　本────サンコー印刷㈱
■装　　　　　丁────ティー・ボーンデザイン事務所

Ⓒ Yuka Tachibana, Linc Educational Resources, Inc 2008, Printed in Japan
検印省略　　落丁・乱丁本はお取り替えいたします。
無断で本書の一部または全部を複写・複製することは禁じられています。
ISBN978－4－88730－873－2